SAYING YES TO JESUS

MY JOURNEY *in the* DEPTHS *of* HIS LOVE

HARVEST SCHOOL 30

JACQUELYN MAY

Saying Yes to Jesus

My Journey in the Depths of His Love—Harvest School 30

Copyright © 2021 – Jacquelyn May

All rights reserved. This book is protected by the copyright laws of the United States of America. No part of this publication may be reproduced, stored in a retrieval system or transmitted in any form or by any means – electronic, mechanical, photocopy, recording or any other – except for brief quotations, without the prior permission of the author.

Cover Design by Rebecca Dias (Paper & Seed)
Cover Photography by Sean Economou (Negev Desert, Israel)

Scripture marked (NKJV) taken from the New King James Version®. Copyright © 1982 by Thomas Nelson. Used by permission. All rights reserved.

Scripture marked (TPT) is taken from The Passion Translation®. Copyright © 2017, 2018, 2020 by Passion & Fire Ministries, Inc. Used by permission. All rights reserved.

ISBN: 979-8-9850892-8-8

sharinghisstoryglobal.com
This book is available on Amazon.com

Endorsements

Saying Yes to Jesus is an exciting journey of discovery of a "hungry heart" that is willing to obey the voice of her Beloved, no matter the price and the sacrifice. Jackie's personal experience will help you, the reader (if you so desire), to follow Jesus in your own walk with Him. By the guidance of the Holy Spirit, you too can make a difference in the life of many that you encounter in this temporary season, as you journey to the Father's house for the eternal glory that is awaiting all of His children.

Mel Tari, Evangelist,
Author, *Like A Mighty Wind*

We highly recommend *Saying Yes to Jesus,* a book about what life looks like when we completely surrender to the King. Jackie has lived out this message of surrender through her own life. Through all the uncertainties she has faced, she has remained steadfast in her devotion to Jesus, trusting Him at every turn no matter the cost. Jackie is a model of what God can do through a yielded life. We endorse her and recommend you dive into this journey of saying yes to Jesus!

Jonathan & Sharon Ngai, Founders
Radiance International, Hollywood House of Prayer

Saying Yes to Jesus is an invitation into a journey that will encourage you, inspire you, bring you awe and wonder, and invite you into a journey of your own. Jackie's simple faith, risk-taking trust, and transforming moments are real, radical, refreshing, and profound. Take the journey!

STEVE & MARCI FISH, SENIOR LEADERS
CONVERGENCE CHURCH, FORT WORTH, TX

The call is going out in this era to whosoever will. Jackie answered with her *yes*. Jackie's story is full of adventure and the joy found in full surrender. No one could do it better. He is the Beautiful Story Writer. Congratulations, Jackie, for writing with authenticity the heights, the depths, the sorrow, and the joy of this great adventure in His Love, His Story. I hope this is just the beginning and a movement of beautiful stories will unfold.

RANDI PEEK, FOUNDER
KATAPAUSE, LLC

This book has the kind of tangible anointing that only occurs when God breathes on an author's writing. I heard the voice of the Lord often as I read, and His presence lingered after I put it down.

I have been at a similar crossroads myself (*"Am I hearing right? Is this really what He's asking?"*) and believe anyone who's ever been in that place can relate to Jackie's journey.

Saying Yes to Jesus is not just a book—it's a spiritual experience.

CHRISTINE CAVITT,
HARVEST SCHOOL ALUMNA, MISSIONARY

Acknowledgements

Thank you to my family for their countless prayers and support throughout my journey. Thank you to my friends, my spiritual family, and church families over the years for praying, encouraging, and cheering me on in the race. Thank you to my mentor, Randi Peek, Katapause LLC, for all of your prayers, guidance, and adventuring with me. Thank you to my editor and friend, Carol Martinez. Thank you to my divinely connected illustrator, Rebecca Dias. Thank you to Heidi and Rolland Baker for hosting Harvest School, which changes the lives of people, families, and shifts nations. Thank you to directors Mama Pamela and Papa Tony for your faithfulness, humor, and being present at the school all of these years. Thank you to Kurt and Brooke for leading our school and stewarding the presence of God, and thank you to all of the Harvest School 30 staff who loved, supported, worshiped, and walked with us on this journey. Thank you to every student who said *yes* to Harvest School 30. It wouldn't have been the same without you. We indeed saw what we've never seen before.

Table of Contents

Introduction   9
Chapter 1:   The Stirring   17
Chapter 2:   The Wooing   29
Chapter 3:   The Provider   37
Chapter 4:   The Arrival in Scotland   49
Chapter 5:   The Truth of God's Love   57
Chapter 6:   The Promised Land   65
Chapter 7:   The Commissioning   73
Chapter 8:   The God of the Breakthrough   81
Chapter 9:   The Bush Bush   97
Chapter 10:   The Perfect Path   109
Chapter 11:   The Rainforest   119
Chapter 12:   The Dance   125
Chapter 13:   The Adventure with God Continues   131
It's Never Too Late to Say YES to Jesus   145

Introduction

I never thought that I would travel outside of the United States, nor did I ever think that I would be a missionary on fire for Jesus. I had become very comfortable in my identity of having a career, a nice place to live, a healthy church community, and saying yes to the things that made me feel like a good Christian.

Before I met Jesus in August 2013, I had lived a life of self-destruction and was searching for anything that could heal my brokenness and help me to feel better. So many years were wasted on partying and doing drugs. I had my share of bad relationships and near-death experiences, and I questioned the meaning of life.

Despite everything, since I grew up Catholic, I continued to go to church on holidays and prayed to God before going to bed. I thought I was going to heaven because I was good. There wasn't much that I knew about God other than him being in heaven, and all I knew about Jesus was that he was hanging on a crucifix above my doorway.

I never felt safe. By the time my parents divorced when I was 16, I was already rebellious. I went through a number of struggles as a child, including abuse from loved ones I should have been able to trust. It wasn't until my mid 20s, after years of self-medicating and realizing counseling and self-help books were only temporary fixes, that I began searching for anything that could bring relief. I had suffered with severe anxiety and panic attacks for years and I was sinking into depression. I wasn't really sure what was happening, but it was one of the scariest feelings that I had ever experienced. I was consumed with fear. I wasn't sure if it was from years of my marijuana use, the abuse I endured from boyfriends, or that the culmination of multiple occurrences of trauma from childhood up until that point had caught up with me. I knew that things in my life needed to change.

Once I was ready to make changes, over the next couple of months, I gradually quit smoking weed and cigarettes and also quit drinking. In the meantime, the anxiety and panic disorder continued to consume my entire life. I would only go places that felt safe and I could only be around people that I knew and was comfortable with. There were many days where I never left my apartment, or I would make my mom stay on the phone with me because I was so scared during the night. If I had a panic attacks driving somewhere, then I would avoid those places altogether. I didn't drive on a highway for at least five years. The doctors recommended that I get on a low-dose antidepressant, but I knew I would only be covering the root issue. Something much deeper was happening. Some days I didn't think I could go on.

I was still somehow able to keep my head above water and manage my apartment, pay bills, and finish my college courses. At the time, I believed it was my own strength and willpower that kept me going. Even though I didn't know Jesus yet, I can look back and see how he protected me and kept me from giving up. Dear friends who lived on a farm gifted me an American Bulldog-Boxer puppy during that time. Rajah kept me busy and alert, and he brought healing and comfort to my heart. I took care of my dog for the next twelve and a half years. The Lord literally saved my life by giving me Rajah.

At the end of Summer 2013, I was interning at a local nonprofit and wanted to give back to the community. I shared an office with a woman named Marcia and we became friends. By then, I was searching for anything that could bring me peace. I was even beginning to entertain the idea of guided meditation. I had been sober around a month and also was beginning to transition from my life as a bartender the past ten years. It wasn't worth forfeiting my sanity anymore. One morning when Marcia and I were alone in our office, she asked me about my relationship with my dad. The next question she asked was if I knew that God was my Father. This stumped me. When people talked to me about God, I often would get defensive. Of course I knew God. I said my prayers at night, was baptized as a baby, and was overall a good person. But the truth was that I did not know him as Father, and I did not have a relationship with Jesus. I only knew God as high up above in heaven and hoped that somehow my prayers might reach him.

She asked if she could pray with me and when she did, something shifted in my heart. When I walked down the hall, I could feel a lightness and peace come over me that I had never experienced before. She gave me the name of a church nearby that carried the presence of God and recommended that I visit it. About a week later, a friend named Megan invited me to that same church. After the service, the pastor asked if there was anyone there who didn't know Jesus and was ready to give their life to him. During the entire service, my heart was being touched and healed, and tears were streaming down my face. I had never heard worship like this before or knew that this was a thing. I was used to kneeling and standing and singing hymns from the book in front of me. I accepted Jesus into my heart that evening and I have never been the same. It was the beginning of my healing journey. Peace, the peace that I had never felt before that I had searched for day in and day out my entire life, was ever present, and God was near.

The next month I hopped on an airplane to visit my aunt in New Mexico and sat next to a woman who soon introduced herself as Joni. She began to share about Jesus with me. I let her know that I had just given my life to him. She wrote on an airplane napkin Psalms 139 and 91. I was absolutely shocked when I found out that God knew me before I was even born and had written every day of my life in his book of remembrance. Since then, these two Psalms have been my go-to scriptures throughout my journey into wholeness, and Joni has become my spiritual mom.

Joni invited me to her small church in Santa Fe that Sunday. It was the first time I saw people filled with the Spirit of God and praying in tongues. Everyone was full of joy and very friendly. When I flew back home, I purchased my first Bible. Joni was the one who discipled me in the Word as I pursued Jesus and attended church each week, learning about my new identity in Christ. A few months later, I got water baptized while they played the song, "I have decided to follow Jesus, no turning back, no turning back." The church gave me a blue bracelet that read "I have decided."

In April 2014, I moved across the United States to the city of Harlingen, Texas. I got my first job as a college graduate and became a program coordinator for a brand-new medical school collaboration. This was a huge step of faith for me since I had never been away from my family for longer than a week. This is where I spent the first three years of my Christ-life, where the Lord built my foundation in him. He surrounded me with a loving church family, generously kind neighbors, and colleagues who were pivotal in shaping my character in Christ. This is also the place where I first experienced the tangible feeling of the Holy Spirit and the prophetic. A lady at church prayed over me and told me that she knew that I was far away from my family, but that God knew me and saw me and would be walking with me every step of the way. The church had thousands of members, and there was no way that she could have known these things about me if they hadn't come straight from God.

In January 2017, God moved me from Harlingen to Fort Worth, Texas, where I accepted a position as the Director of Faculty Affairs for another new medical school collaboration. I could hardly believe that after three short years in the medical field, I had received the favor to step into such a high-level role and position. Here, the Lord began to build my life on a more mature level in him. I attended Convergence Church. My pastors at that time, Steve and Marci Fish, were very close with Heidi and Rolland Baker. This is where I first began to hear about Iris Global. While at Convergence, I attended a school of supernatural ministry and learned about hearing the voice of God, five-fold ministry and the gifts of the Spirit, including healing, prophecy and words of knowledge. I began to see the miraculous healing power of Jesus through miracles and deliverance on the streets. I knew that God was slowly preparing me to leave the medical school and step out into full-time ministry and into the fullness of who he called me to be.

One night I went to a special service at my church where Will Hart, Iris's CEO and a radical missionary, would be speaking. At the end of his message, he called me out of the congregation and asked me to stand up. He began to prophesy that he saw service all over me and that I was a rescuer. He even saw me rescuing women from the streets and breaking the spirit of suicide off of people's lives. He said that I was going to answer the call and say yes when no one else would. This call that he spoke into me was the beginning of my abandoned life journey that catapulted me into full time ministry and attending Iris Global Harvest School 30.

A month later, I stepped away from the medical school and said yes to a position at a nonprofit for women and children when no one else was willing. Downtown Fort Worth was full of people that were homeless and the need for Jesus to be in that place was great. God reminded me a couple weeks later when I was running on the treadmill that I was to say yes when everyone else said no. I love how the Holy Spirit is the one who brings things to remembrance. I knew that God wanted to heal the broken and bring restoration to that place. For the next seven months while in that position, I was humbled, stretched, broken, healed, used, pressed, and loved by the precious little kids and people in the city. There was immense favor from the CEO and bosses as I served their vision. This was the preparation mission before the main mission, the fire before the go, that prepared me for the inner city and the nations.

Even though I had been saved and 'free' for a number of years, I had established a 'play it safe' routine. Even though my journey had already been one of great faith, it had become comfortable to do life with my church community, co-workers and neighbors. I loved living in a brand-new apartment and the luxuries of life. The presence of God was very strong at my church and I was part of many prayer groups. I finally felt content with where I was in life.

It was at that time when God called me to step out of everything that I knew to walk on the water with him again. This really tested my heart to the point that I had never been tested before. It was more than just saying *yes* and being obedient to the call of coming away with him. It was trusting him every step of the way and leaving family and friends behind again. It was deciding to follow Jesus into the deeper waters and not turning back. I never could have dreamed or imagined the plans that God had for me. "For I know the plans I have for you declares the Lord, plans to prosper you and not to harm you, plans to give you a hope and a future" (Jeremiah 29:11 NIV). It has been a wild ride and continues to get better and better each day. Thanks for coming along on my adventure at Harvest School 30. My hope is that you would be encouraged and inspired to give Jesus your *yes* and to step into your calling and mission field that he is asking you to join him in.

Chapter 1

THE STIRRING

It was the fall of 2018. I was living in Fort Worth, Texas and going through a season of feeling like there was more. It wasn't discontentment, but there was a stirring inside of me that wanted to know Jesus more and pursue the call of evangelism. A friend of mine had mentioned Evangelist Daniel Kolenda who had an organization called Christ for All Nations and was serving under Reinhard Bonnke. As I was researching, I saw that he was hosting a weeklong evangelism school training in January 2019. I decided to apply for the school. All I wanted to do was share about the goodness of God and lead others out of darkness and into a relationship with Jesus. A few weeks later, I was accepted to the school and flew to Orlando.

I've learned that God always has something so much bigger that exceeds all expectations of what I think something is going to look like. As soon as I walked in the door, the presence of God was all around. The school was filled with worship, teaching, equipping, and servant leadership like I had never experienced before. I learned to cultivate Jesus in the secret place and how everything flows from the place of spending time with him. I stayed with three other girls from around the world and there were many different nations represented.

The week flew by and we were all excited for the final impartation night when the leaders would pray over each one of us. My heart was positioned and open to receive whatever word God had for me. When Daniel Kolenda walked past me and prayed, the tangible presence of God came over me and I fell back onto the floor. I couldn't stop laughing. This carried on for a while. I was still conscious and could hear everything going on, but something was stirring deep inside of my spirit. Students were standing up for more prayer, but I couldn't move. I didn't want to miss what God had for me in that moment. Daniel walked past me a second time and I reached my hand out and he said, "more fire." I immediately went into a vision of a place that was very green, like a rainforest, and I saw trees, sand, a body of water and an elephant. The people there were from some kind of a tribe. I felt like I was in another dimension. I still can't explain what happened to me that night. I went from laughing full of the joy of the Lord, to crying and receiving God's heart, to visions of green land. This school was one of the most special places that I've been honored to attend. By the time I left, I was different.

After returning home from the evangelism school, I had no idea what was next. I was working a full-time job at the nonprofit for women, locked into both apartment and car leases, and had many other bills and responsibilities. I had lived on my own for over 15 years, yet I had never traveled out of the country other than to Canada. After I prayed and pondered, I felt like there was a burden in my heart that God needed to release, but I didn't know what it was. What was this stirring inside of me? I felt like I was supposed to go somewhere—but where? I sat before God and waited for his answer.

At the evangelism school, I had connected with Claire, a girl from Australia who told me about an online class called "The School of the Secret Place" that Brian Guerin was teaching. She shared how, after taking this class, she began to experience the supernatural and encounter God in a new way. We also talked about stewardship of prophetic words and stepping out by faith.

I took Claire's advice about stewardship and signed up for Brian's class. During that time, God spoke to me in ways I had never experienced before. I began to dream dreams that I remembered and recorded throughout the night. I was getting words of knowledge for people that I met on the street and God was giving me eyes to see them the way he saw them—through eyes of love. The miracles of God moving in boldness and power in my everyday life were becoming very real, and his love was washing over me and changing me to be more like him.

The church I belonged to in Fort Worth, Convergence, is mission partners with Iris Global and the pastors, Steve and Marci Fish, are close friends with Heidi and Rolland Baker. They always shared about Iris and their yearly trips to Mozambique. When I listened, it made me want to go too, but at the time it was impossible. I started looking up opportunities on the Iris Global website and saw they were getting ready to host a Harvest School 30 starting in June. Usually, they would have this school every year in Pemba, but this time, due to new Visa restrictions, it would be a traveling school and completely different than the previous ones. Instead, it was going to take place consecutively in Scotland, Israel, and Madagascar. I had no idea where Madagascar even was until I took out a map to find it. The first time I Googled it, I clicked on the images and saw a picture of a bright green rainforest with a body of water and sand. I read about the nation and saw that it was an island off of the Indian ocean, mostly inhabited by tribes. I felt the nudging of the Holy Spirit kindly remind me of the vision that I had when I was on the ground during the impartation night at the evangelism school. Since I was pretty content with my nice life, church community, friends, and apartment, I wondered what God was saying about this. I didn't want to run and take off for two months for the school and then come back to nothing. But interestingly, both my apartment lease and car lease were also ending in June, so I had to decide whether or not to renew them. It was the same month the school would begin.

The next Sunday at church, Pastor Steve had us close our eyes and imagine that God, our Father, was writing us a blank check and handing it to us. As we were meditating on this, we envisioned God as our creator and provider of all things. We were encouraged to drink deep in this moment of dreaming with God. I imagined a mission trip in another country and that someday I would even take part of building safe homes for children. I decided that was what I would do with the blank check—rescue children.

When I arrived home from church that afternoon, I was really excited and feeling great from being with Jesus. I grabbed my laptop and carried it to the couch and sat down. I Googled "Madagascar" again. In that moment, the Holy Spirit came over me, and my whole body began to shake. I knew right then that there was definitely a connection and that God was trying to show me something about the Harvest School 30. In my mind, it was impossible for me to even think about doing this because of the short timeline. By now it was

April, and the applications had been open since January. I took this request to God and decided to start taking some faith steps forward to see where he was leading.

Iris has a list of required books to read before you can attend the school. This was another concern since the time frame was short. I signed into Amazon and bought the books because whether I decided to do the school or not, I knew that Heidi's testimonies and missionary stories would be well worth the read.

I was both excited and a bit scared that God could be asking me to do this kind of a move. I reached out to my friend Claire from the evangelism school and asked her if she knew anyone who would be attending Iris Harvest School 30, since she is part of Iris Australia. She asked me if I remembered Fred, whom I had also met at the evangelism school. She shared that he and his entire family were going to join Harvest School 30. I couldn't believe it! This was yet another confirmation of God leading the adventure ahead.

A few mornings later, I met my mentor and our mutual friend for coffee. Her son was currently on staff at Iris Global. At the end of our meeting, I mentioned that I was considering applying for Harvest School. She said to me, "When I walked in this morning, I looked at you from across the coffee shop and thought, *Jackie looks just like an Iris leader.*" She mentioned that she never looked at people like this or labeled them, but she had been praying that morning and asked God to give her rose-colored glasses so she could see people the way that he sees him. I decided after that day and multiple other nudges that I was going to apply for the school.

Applying for the school was probably the easiest part of the journey. I completed the application over the course of a few days. Part of the application was to make a video on why I wanted to attend. I followed through, even though I wasn't quite sure other than the vision I had; international missions weren't really on my heart at the time. I also shared how the tangible presence of the Holy Spirit was undeniable when I would look at photos of the kids in Madagascar. I finished my video, application, and submitted my two references. At this point, I knew I could back out if I really wanted to. I hadn't invested any money yet.

God was going to have to make himself really clear to me because this was bigger than anything that I could do in my own strength. I loved my life in Fort Worth. Was I ready to give it all up for a two-month mission trip? There was a lot of confusion in discerning where God wanted me to be because I was also feeling strongly that he could be sending me back to Ohio where my family was. I knew that whatever I chose could change the entire trajectory of my life. The voice of confusion was clouding my understanding and peace. At times I would ask myself, *Am I being obedient, or am I trying to find my own way and figure it out?* This can happen when you have a strong personality and try to make sense of the things of God. Coming from a rebellious background and reverting back to orphan ways at times, I always had to weigh my own motives and make sure it was Holy Spirit and not me doing something and calling it Holy Spirit. What would it look like to lay my life in Fort Worth completely down and get rid of everything I owned? What would it cost to lay it all down and go? With previous opportunities like the School of Evangelism, I knew that if I didn't go, I was going to miss the path. If I decided not to go to Harvest School, I felt there would be other opportunities, but did I need to go on this trip in order to become the woman he had predestined me to be and to carry out his purposes on earth as it is in heaven? I constantly had to pray against the spirit of fear in the decision-making process, well aware that the enemy prowls around, seeking those who he can devour. I asked myself if, perhaps, the fact that it was "Heidi's School" was the main draw. God reminded me about the shortcuts I'd taken in life because of time, money, and fear, and that he really wanted me to take his perfect path on this decision.

Every day, I would check the status of my application. Yet at the same time, I was trying to convince myself why I needed to move back home. I had been away from my family for years, my mom was retiring, sister had a baby, and my stepdad needed help with his business. Added to that, there was a small Iris-based church there that I really enjoyed, called Frontline International. They were inviting me on a mission trip to Mozambique with their team that summer that would be taking place at the same time as Harvest School. It made a lot of sense for me to move my stuff back to Ohio, join in with this local missions-based church and inner-city outreach, and travel around the world. This sounded like the golden ticket.

The more I read about Harvest School 30, the more I doubted that this was what God had for me. There was no way that I could spend over $10,000 on a two-month school. The school was $4500, and the flights could be up to $5000 plus spending money for the trip. I wasn't ready to give up my apartment and end my lease; it was the best place that I had ever lived. It was in the perfect location, surrounded by restaurants, trails, shops, and people who I loved. It was so convenient. The past couple of years that I had spent in that apartment had given me so much joy for many reasons. I had met many beautiful people. My beloved companion, my dog Rajah, had recently passed away, and I had spent the last waking breaths with him there. I also enjoyed spending time with my dad's side of the family where we made many memories. I had not spent much time with them since childhood. It was a holy house—a dwelling for the Lord. My safe place. I loved my car. How was I going to go without a car? I also would have to make the decision of leaving my job very soon. They were putting some pressure on me about going to a conference that summer, and I needed to purchase my plane ticket soon in order to go. I didn't feel right spending the nonprofit's money if God was going to move me somewhere else.

The longer my application took to go through, the more I wanted to back out of it. The fear around me was becoming too great. My analytical mind was getting in the way and I felt that it was a huge risk. My mentor kept asking me if I could imagine all that I would miss out on if I didn't follow God on this one. Others would ask me if there was another Harvest School that I could attend in a different season. My family was very fearful of me doing mission work in another country. There was so much opposition. I was cautious about who I shared with and the counsel that I sought. I wanted to hear God's voice and his heart for this. There were many options, but only one was the story that he had written about me. I was determined to seek his perfect will and to choose his best for me.

During this time, my dreams were more vivid than ever before. They were like a roadmap on where I was to go and what I was to do. I'd never seen numbers so clearly and impressions that God used to speak to me about this season, truly ordering every step.

In one particular dream that I had, I was at a table that was set up on a platform in a home. You had to walk up a couple of steps inside the house to reach it. An abundance of food, including steak and breakfast French toast, was being passed around. Behind me was a counter like a rental car business. I was complaining because I was driving around in this rental jeep, and I couldn't see over the dashboard since I am short. My old boss was working behind the counter, and she was getting ready to give me a new car. She gave me a truck. I was completely horrified by the truck, because I already couldn't see out of the jeep. Then, one of my friends and my pastor's wife came out from this back room, both laughing. I asked, "Where did you guys just come from?" and they said a "disconnect" meeting. This was really strange to me because I was currently on the connect team at my church. In the same dream, the scene changed, and I was laughing and so excited at this wonderful feast that I was at with new friends at the table. I packed my leftover food up in a Styrofoam box, but then I somehow misplaced it. A friend, Kendra, got down on the ground with me and began to help me look for my box. She was very caring and kind in the dream.

The next morning, I woke up to a text from my pastor's wife, asking if I wanted to have breakfast that weekend with her and Kendra to talk about an upcoming vision for the church and the city. We met up at a restaurant that had the exact same French toast that I had dreamt about. When we finished eating, we asked for to-go boxes and they were Styrofoam! I felt a disconnect from the meeting. I supported all that was being shared, but I felt that my spirit was heading to another place. I realized that the dream I had was a prophetic act of God seating me at a new table with new people. Regarding the Jeep and truck, even though I felt deep in over my head and couldn't see over the dash, God knew exactly what he was giving me to drive.

About a week later, I had a dream that my seat at church was taken. In the dream, we were in our old church auditorium called the

CAC and someone was in my seat. I had to sit in the back, and I had dozens of African children hanging around and climbing all over me. Those were two different confirmations that the next season of my life would not take place at my current church. The confirmation that came from the dreams was stirring faith inside of me regarding his perfect plan for my life.

I started seeing the numbers 330 and 648 on everything. Harvest School 30 dates were June 3-July 30 (330). For weeks, the clock would constantly show 648 every time I looked at it. I wasn't sure yet what this was about since 648 was my mom's address. One day, I was walking to my apartment complex's office, and a newspaper was thrown right in front of the door. Someone had written in black marker, "330." There had to be some kind of connection. Just like prophecy, I would take every dream, thought, and word back to God to see what he was saying about it.

Meanwhile, in spite of the wrestling, I was beginning to hear God's voice. Heidi and Rolland's books were also stirring so much faith inside of me during this waiting season with the Lord. I really enjoyed *Compelled by Love*, *There is Always Enough*, *Visions Beyond the Veil* and the Harvest School Workbooks. The testimonies of God's faithfulness and how he always provides even in the most impossible situations stirred my heart to want to go deeper with the Lord. My application was still pending a final reference that they had not yet received. The pending of the application was purposeful. It was preparing my heart for the yes.

I woke up the next morning and checked my email. I had received a notification and welcome letter that my Harvest School application had been approved! In an instant, all my remaining reservations disappeared. My heart was exploding with gladness and joy was overflowing from my spirit. I opened up the manual and skimmed through the 29 pages of extensive information regarding next steps and what to expect. The manual included a dress code section for the three countries which consisted of everything from winter layers to sleeping bags. I had never gone camping—let alone to a third world country. There was also a section that mentioned the vaccine requirements and Malarial meds that we needed to enter the countries. Shots were something that I was not a fan of and couldn't recall getting any since I was five, holding my mom's hand.

That same week, I had another dream where I saw the letters IRIS blown up really big like balloons. The number of the school—Harvest 30—really resonated in my heart with God's divine timing. God reminded me that I got saved when I was 29 years old and started in ministry at 30. I was also 30 when I was baptized and filled with the Holy Spirit. Jesus began his ministry at age 30. Harvest School 30 was going to be the first traveling school to Scotland, Israel, and Madagascar. There were so many options but only one yes that the Lord wanted. Would my life work out if I joined the Ohio church and went on their mission trip? Sure. Would I somehow figure out my new life back in Ohio at home with family? Possibly. But I knew after these confirmations that God was leading me to attend the school.

As I journaled and prayed, I realized how often I had put God into my comfortable box which still included stepping out and trying new things, but I had never actually let him completely break the box. My box was marked with scratches, chips and dents, but it wasn't totally broken. Was I ready to be completely broken and to walk on the water? At times I had felt very lonely following him. However, he always met me in those places, wrapping his loving arms around me, comforting and filling me with his grace to be able to go on another day. He knows how to get us exactly where he wants us to go.

I was a bit vulnerable because this one decision was going to completely change the entire course of my life. I would write and tell God, *I'll say yes to whatever you have for me.* So much easier said than done. But I made the vow that my life is solely to follow Jesus and to be obedient to him. My heart broke at the thought of how many people in this world still don't know him, and that they will spend an eternity away from him. This decision wasn't just about me; people's souls were at stake. People who had been in bondage for years could actually be set free because of my obedience to Jesus.

Chapter 2

THE WOOING

In order to do the Iris trip, I have to have somewhere to stay when I come back in August ... I had so many racing thoughts and responsibilities flashing through my mind. Do I put my stuff into a storage unit, or move it back to Ohio? My car lease is up, do I sign another one or extend my current lease so I will have a car when I return? But then, do I really see myself paying so much money for my car to sit in a driveway while I'm gone? How in the world am I going to pay for this trip? It's going to be close to $10,000 dollars. What about my job? They told me to talk to them before I decide to leave because they might be able to offer me a higher position and more pay. Maybe I can even take a sabbatical and go back to work after this trip is over. My church is opening up opportunities for me to partner with them. Should I stick around and just do something here in Fort Worth? How will I know if I am to move back to Ohio or not?

All of these decisions were huge, and there was a lot that I needed to pray through. I started making my lists and getting things prepared to potentially pack up my entire apartment. My prayer was, *God, please open up someone's home when I return from Harvest School if this is what you have for me.*

While praying and waiting on the Lord, I was beginning to have more of a deep peace that transcended all understanding. Things were becoming clearer. I asked God what his heart for my family was at that time too. I felt guilty, almost like I was leaving them behind while they were looking forward to me moving back home. Years prior, the Lord had spoken to me about my family being part of the mission field and to spend time and the money visiting and loving them well. Over the years, he has kept my family close when he moves me from place to place.

There is always a cost when following Jesus. I asked him all these questions, and he was so gracious to answer. During this time, God really showed me how I must not be shaken by people, their actions/reactions, how they treat me, what they say or if they show me affection. I need to stand in the promises of the Lord because he cares. I also believed that God wanted to heal my entire heart, setting me free of past pain, feelings, and memories.

I could see how working at the nonprofit had healed and humbled my heart in so many ways. It broke me down to my knees; I was placed in dark atmospheres and chaos, but God picked me up, shifted me, and set me back on his rock. I believe that healing had to happen during each season for the places and call of where he was taking me. I longed to share the good news about Jesus with everyone and for them to experience his love. I didn't want my own desires to hinder the perfect plan.

As I continued with my preparations and God continued his work in me, whenever I shared with others about the opportunity to join Harvest School 30, the Spirit of God would take my breath away, and I would begin to cry with no explanation or words. The love of God would come over me and all I could do was surrender. Each day was ultimate submission under the Lord and laying it all down at his feet. As I stated in a journal entry at the time: *That's what it means to be mission-minded. Laying my life down every day isn't easy and it is a continual dying to self, but there is joy in the overcoming and persevering, no matter how hard it is. Jesus paid the price for it all.*

Before discovering Iris Global, I didn't specifically have a heart to go to the nations, mostly because I saw God move and use me in my local neighborhood, apartment complex, workplace, supermarkets, and with my family. But if he wanted to take me to the nations, then I knew that he had something really big for me there. I knew that God was going to give me the next step as he always had done before. I was sick of trying to figure it out on my own, but the closer I drew to him and encountered him in the secret place, the clearer his heart became for me. I heard God speak such sweet words as the Triune—Father, Son, and Holy Spirit. He told me to come and delight in him, to feast on his word and his goodness.

I wanted to finish my time in Fort Worth well because I knew that finishing well matters. My workload at the nonprofit was starting to wrap up. I had remained until we had our annual Ask Event which was focused on bringing awareness and ending homelessness for women and children. During this season at work, I was able to build relationships with three fantastic women and their children; each represented a life restored from poverty to possibility. The media team and I followed these families for months, filming and capturing their daily lives. One of the ways God healed my heart was by revealing himself through these women whose lives had been redeemed and restored. Before, they had been homeless, abused, neglected, and left for dead. I could relate closely with them on so many levels from the years that I had been living in darkness and was lost. It reminded me that if it hadn't been for my family, I too would have been homeless.

Even though my apartment lease wasn't ending until June, in order to not pay thousands in fees, I had to give a 60-day advance notice. I didn't feel comfortable putting in my notice without having anywhere to go and still wasn't sure I was ready to let go of my apartment yet. This was my life and saying goodbye was not easy. I meditated on Romans 8:28 constantly. *God, I know that you are working all things together for good because I love you and have been called according to your purpose.*

One afternoon I was walking up my back steps to the gym and noticed about eight moving bins that were left by the trash shoot. I didn't know if someone still needed them or was throwing them away. The next day I went to the gym and they were still there. I called the apartment manager and asked if I could have them since they were unclaimed. I figured they would come in handy eventually for a move, especially since they were sturdy plastic with wheels. I made multiple trips up and down the steps stacking them in front of my back door. I glanced down at the container on the top, and in all caps, it said IRIS inside of a heart. I couldn't believe it. There were Sterlite containers underneath and some random ones, but I had never heard of the Iris storage containers before. This had to be God. I took a few photos just to make myself believe this was real. The cloud was moving, and I had the choice to move with it, or to stay in my comfort zone.

The more that I read the books that were assigned, the more the stirring of my spirit would roar up inside, giving me confidence to excel into the new without borders. I read Rees Howell's book, *Intercessor* and saw how much faith Rees had to trust God and do exactly what God said. Rees would get comfortable many times in his life and see the favor of the Lord working, but then God would ask him to shift, and Rees would shift immediately, no matter how silly it looked.

As I continued going through the Iris manual where the many expectations, instructions, and requirements were laid out, it was overwhelming. I would have to lie down on the couch just to process it all. I told God there was no way I could do this. Pack for three countries and three climates for two months in just one suitcase and a carry-on? Besides, how in the world was I going to finish all of the required books and also pack up my entire apartment before leaving?

I asked him to send people to walk with me on the journey and to help me be a good steward with my finances. Focusing on money always makes me hesitate—I tend to count the cost more than the rewards of following him and giving him my heart. Yet there was no way around the issue … both the $10,000 for the trip and provision afterward. When I was driving one day, I heard the Lord say to me, *I can take that $10,000 and turn it into 100,000.* I took this as a two-fold promise from God. He wasn't only talking $100,000 dollars; I believed he was also referring to 100,000 souls. A double harvest.

I took a personal day from work that Friday to relax at my pool where I could just breath again. When I showed up at the pool, my neighbor who lived across the street was hanging out. She hadn't been to the pool in weeks and just so happened to have the day off as well. This was a divine appointment from the Lord. I explained a little bit of what was going on in my life, and she told me that she had gone on many mission trips and was getting ready to head to Mexico the following month. I could feel the peace of God as she reassured me that even though it seemed overwhelming, it was all very doable. She offered to walk me through the manual and show me what I needed to buy, where to purchase it, and how to get it all together. In that moment, I felt the grieving of my spirit start to leave and the spirit of joy began to rise up in my heart—it was the same feeling I had the day that I saw the initial acceptance email from Iris. This woman was an answered prayer and a vessel of God's goodness.

Sunday morning at church, I felt all through the service that God wanted my yes. I even kept seeing the letters in huge print like bubbled up balloons again, "SAY YES." I sadly wasn't quite ready yet to give him my yes even though he so graciously asked.

Monday morning came around and I was working on my Harvest workbook which was part of the mandatory reading. As soon as I turned the page in my workbook, I read the paragraph that talked about God's favor and grace. It said that when God's favor is on us, it looks so wild and out of the box, but he gives us the grace to walk it out. The next paragraph then stated, "God just wants your yes." All sorts of thoughts began stirring in my mind: *He just called me to the front to give him my yes, and clearly, I wasn't obedient, and now it's Monday morning and he is reiterating it to me again.* Jesus was wooing me to come away with him.

Later that night when I got home from work and Bible study, I felt led to worship. I had these really cool ceiling speakers that could blast worship throughout my entire apartment as I encountered the Lord in the secret place. As I worshiped, I sat on the floor and began to thank him and praise him. I felt the weight and the glory of the Lord and I lay back on the floor. As soon as I lay back, I began to laugh hysterically and felt drunk in the Spirit, by myself, on my kitchen floor. I couldn't stop laughing because the spirit of joy was upon me and God was there. I was stuck to the ground and couldn't even lift my arms. It was such a fun night of encounter as he met me where I was. And I gave him my *yes*. I knew that whatever it looked like, that I was laying it all down and was going to press forward until I heard *stop*. I was going to go.

"If it means going home after Harvest School, staying in Fort Worth, whatever it is, I say YES to you God. For you are God, and you are worthy of my life and all that I have!" I cried out.

I thanked him for all of the confirmations, directions, dreams, visions, impressions, divine appointments and encounters he had given me. I also thanked him for the encouragement and comfort he continued to give me throughout the process, the friends he sent, and for the prayers that moved mountains. I thanked him for the freedom to choose, and grace and favor in the journey. I was so excited to partner with him.

Chapter 3

THE PROVIDER

I turned in my apartment 60-day notice by faith, trusting I would have somewhere to come back to when I returned. When I walked home from the apartment office, I cried. The same heaviness that I had when my dog Rajah had died 6 months prior came over me because I was saying goodbye to a place where we shared so many memories. I knew this was part of the preparation process because I never could have left Rajah for two months. I prayed for continued peace and clarity, believing that God's plans were good and that he was for me and not against me. He reminded me in that moment that I was actually content with where I was in life. I wasn't trying to run away or do something rebellious or get out of my current situation and responsibilities. I was simply answering what he was calling me to do. I kept hearing the phrase: new shoes, expansion, multiplication.

After I was accepted for Harvest School, I was added to their social media page. I saw an opening paragraph where it asked for people who were going to attend to share where they were from. I saw that a girl named Rebecca who only lived 30 minutes from me was attending. She was Harvest School alumna and loved helping other first-time missionaries. We were able to meet up and connect at Starbucks to get to know one another. I had asked God before I even applied if he would give me a travel buddy to go with. I knew God had answered yet another prayer!

During worship the following Sunday, I had a vision after giving my *yes* where I was marrying Jesus. He held out a robe as I walked down the aisle and when I walked up the stairs, he wrapped his heavy, soft, purple-colored robe around me. There were tons of jewels and Jesus said to me, "Here is my robe of righteousness." I immediately knew that he was referring to Isaiah 61:10 (NKJV):

> I will greatly rejoice in the Lord,
> My soul shall be joyful in my God;
> For He has clothed me with the garments of salvation,
> He has covered me with the robe of righteousness,
> As a bridegroom decks himself with ornaments,
> And as a bride adorns herself with her jewels.

It was a celebration. He was adorning me and clothing me in his beauty filled with love and grace.

Over the next few days, God continued to remind me of that impression and deeply spoke to my heart connecting what was going on in the natural with what he was doing in the Spirit. It was a process of preparation. A wedding can be very expensive and include a lot of planning and prep work. Brides are very excited but at the same time, nerves are running all over the place in the decision-making process. There is anticipation of what to expect and many questions regarding whether she has chosen the right dress, cake, people to invite and more. She knows that God has called her to marry this person, but there are still so many unknowns and natural fears that come with choosing and taking such a huge step of trust into a lifelong commitment and covenant.

Usually, there is also considerable give-and-take that happens during the process of engagement in preparation of getting married. You might need to clear out your house and get rid of things that will not be going with you to the next place with your husband. Maybe you still live at your parents' house and have never lived with anyone else before. Or maybe, you've been married before or had a really bad experience living with a parent or roommate. Then, once you're married, you become one, and it's no longer all about you and God. It's you, God and your husband.

God was showing me all of these things through his eyes. I was getting married to Jesus in this season, and in that, I needed to get rid of a lot of things that weren't coming with me to the next. There was going to be a lot of sacrifice and a very expensive adventure ahead, but the reward of getting to marry him and becoming robed in his righteousness was going to be worth every moment, every penny, and every breath of my life. He was courting me during this time in the sweetest way; kindly taking me by the hand into the unknown places and reassuring me that everything was going to be okay. I thanked him for choosing me as his bride.

The next week, I kept reciting over myself, "The Lord is my shepherd. He is my counselor and my strength." It was during this time of rapid, expensive, decision making that I sought God as my counselor, and he comforted me in the way that only a true friend could. He was more than enough, and he wanted to show himself faithful in every single detail. He showered me with divine favor by sending people at just the right time to comfort me and talk me off of the edge, and he even gave me favor at the doctor's office. I was petrified of getting shots and vaccines for the first time since childhood, but knew it was one more thing I had to do. The doctor billed all of my shots under routine vaccines since I hadn't had them since I was young, and then he gave me his number just in case I had any issues or needed more medication. I even had favor at the pharmacy with the Malarial meds that were costing people hundreds of dollars. They had the exact number of pills that I needed to cover my entire trip and with insurance they only came to $35.

I made the first financial step and paid my registration fee for Iris of $400. I went to the pastors of my church and received their blessing; they then did the kindest thing and let me raise support for my mission trip through the church. A couple of years before, I would have never thought that at some point I would give away my belongings, live without a salary, and get rid of my car and place to live, but now I knew that God asked me to partner with him in this and to invite other people on board who would want to support the mission and sow financially and prayerfully into my trip.

Fundraising is a full-time job in itself. It involves a lot of communication, interfacing, thank you notes, updates, and financial database tracking. All of this was in addition to my other ten to-do lists of what it would take to move out, including handling and transitioning finances while out of the country for two months, turning in my leased vehicle, and somehow packing and moving all of my stuff somewhere that was still unknown. This was also in the midst of buying clothes for three seasons, (since I would be experiencing three seasons in two months) along with other hiking and adventure gear, plus purging and selling everything I no longer needed or wanted. I also needed to finish reading and completing the Iris books and training manuals. I look back now and say it was only with God that I was able to pull any of this off. I am absolutely amazed at how he worked it all out.

I typed out my financial support letter and had a colleague proof it before I sent it out to everyone. God put a list of people on my heart that I had the pleasure of doing life with over the previous years who I thought would want to partner with me. Some were Spirit-filled believers, some ex-colleagues, family, and some friends who always believed in my purpose and destiny of helping others. I typically would never ask for money or support since I lived a very private life. I had also been independent with a job for many years and had supported myself financially. Having to ask others for support exposed a lot of pride in these areas and showed me where I needed to lay it all down in complete trust and abandonment unto him, the provider of my life who desires to be part of everything.

I contacted the travel agent who was assigned by Iris to book our flights, and I told her that I wanted to be on Rebecca's initial flight to Scotland. I was shocked when she informed me of the price, which was much higher than the amount Rebecca had paid. The school was already $4500, so how in the world was I supposed to pay almost $5000 more, just so I could be on Rebecca's flight?

In my spirit, I heard the Lord say, *Do not cut corners*. I wasn't really sure what that meant, so I waited. I was getting nervous about flights. I had wanted to fly with my new friend Rebecca, but she had planned to fly through Ethiopia to Madagascar, and if I were to take the same flight, I would need a Yellow Fever vaccine. Reluctantly, I scheduled the vaccine appointment—but when I got to the doctor's office I didn't feel right about the situation. I remembered God's words, don't cut corners. The nurse kindly agreed to wait while I called the travel agent. After some hesitation and difficulty working through flight options, the travel agent miraculously found a flight through Johannesburg instead of Ethiopia—and it was $1,000 cheaper! And I would still be able to fly with Rebecca from Dallas to Scotland. I knew it was God's favor.

During Easter, I let my family know that I wasn't going to be coming back to Ohio to live. It was like every closed door brought a sense of peace and confirmation. Still, I had many questions like, *Where do I keep my stuff and where do I live when I return? Do I send my stuff to Ohio or keep it here in storage? Where am I going to live when I get back?*

The more anticipation and nervousness I was getting regarding this trip, the more the Lord began to show me that this was a time of sanctification and setting apart before I became his bride in the way I had seen in my vision. My family and others blessed me financially and were supporting my decision to go on this adventure.

There's something very powerful about thanking God in advance and releasing the prophetic blessing over your future. We are to call things into existence according to the way that God sees them. I began to thank him for choosing me. I thanked him in advance for the girls that I would be rooming with during Harvest School and for my outreach team. *Thank you for the people that are going to be on my Harvest School 30 trip. Thank you for comforting me when I face the uncomfortable and healing me from motion sickness and vertigo as I travel on these buses. Thank you for supporting me and giving me courage to ask people to give, to leave my life, and to follow you. It's really hard. But I know that you are so worth it and that every time I say yes to you it is worth it. You have delivered me from so much darkness and have turned my mourning into joy. I am forever grateful for your love, mercy, and comfort that you have given me.*

I looked back at all the blessings I had received just in the past few days. I had favor at my apartment complex and even the office managers sowed into my trip. All of my shots for the trip were taken care of and I didn't have to get the Yellow Fever vaccine. I got my flights for $1,000 cheaper. I put in my notice at work and they had a going-away party for me. God opened a door for me to store my stuff at a local storage unit down the street from my apartment. They gave me ten free boxes, a free lock, and the first month for free. My unit was number 7 which means completion or spiritual perfection. My Honda passed the leasing company's inspection even though someone swiped my back bumper, and they didn't end up charging me for anything. I raised $3300 dollars in the first week and a half. I was absolutely blown away. I was shouting unto the Lord.

In the midst of it all, I attended Light the Fire Conference in Toronto which my friend Sharon had me invited to. While there, I had some significant encounters with the Lord, confirmed words and promises, and divine appointments. At the end of the night the attendees could receive prayer and impartation from some of the pioneers in the faith. I received many impartations from fathers in the faith who had deliverance ministries and ministries all over the world. Daniel Kolenda was there and stopped to say hello and prayed for me again. I heard God say, *double portion, double anointing, and double harvest* over my life. The fire of God fell in that place.

This short international trip to Canada also made me realize other things I needed to do before leaving for two months. I recognized I was under-packed and under-prepared. God was working everything together for good. I'm thankful for Iris's manual with all of the information on what you need to do in preparation for the Harvest School. As the days went on, I began to adjust more and more with being in the moment and enjoying each day for what it was instead of being stressed out with all of the unknowns.

On my last day of work, I got to take my favorite guy, who was homeless and lived out back of the nonprofit and his dog to lunch. God had used him and his dog, Chuckie, to bring reconciliation to my heart after losing Rajah months back. I look back at my time at this nonprofit and realize it was all part of God's plan. Not only was I able to help many people each day, but God also healed my heart from many wounds from the past that I didn't even realize were still buried inside. Driving home that night I heard Holy Spirit say, well done. During my time there I saw an immediate shift from some staff leaving and management bringing in an entirely new staff, to friendships and love, to children being loved on and prayed for and even the name of Jesus being spoken in our business meetings.

The following Monday night, I attended my small group, or micro church, and shared about Harvest School 30. It's a blessing to be surrounded by a great community of believers who can encourage and confirm the call of God on your life. I still had no idea where I was going to be staying when I returned from the school, but that night, God highlighted Carol and Daryl who are a loving, older couple who attended my church and were hosting the micro church in their home that evening. As soon as I got there, it felt like an oasis retreat. Could there be an open door for me to stay with them? The Bible clearly says to, "Ask and you shall receive, knock and the door be opened, and seek and you will find him according to his will." The worst thing they could say if I asked was no. I asked Carol in private that evening if they would be willing to host me when I returned in August. Carol got back to me and said yes. This was affirming and confirming to me as I knew the Lord had highlighted this restful place to me.

I connected with the moving guy who moved my stuff into my apartment when I first arrived in Fort Worth and would now be helping me over two years later move my stuff to storage. He was a Christian and we shared many stories about salvation in our families, inner city evangelism, and also prayed together. I could see God connecting all of the dots. His favor was all over this decision and he granted me favor with others.

My prayer life was increasing as I continued to pray in the Spirit daily. As I was being stretched it was like my legs were going higher and my feet were becoming deeply rooted. I had to call on the name of Jesus constantly and invite him into each thing that I was doing, even something as small as how to pack a certain box. He is the God of detail. I prayed grace over every area of my life and for the presence of peace to overcome me before I left for the trip. I continually thanked him in the midst of everything that I was facing because in the praise and thanksgiving, it brought rest to my soul. I repented of all fear and worry.

The following Sunday at church, I kept having a picture in my mind of a man that had come to me through visions during the prior weeks. I asked the Lord, *Is this my husband or is this a picture of my Jesus?* That day at church, my pastor was teaching about looking directly into the eyes of Jesus and staying on focused on him. He gave the example of playing tennis and how our eyes need to be so focused on the tennis ball that we can't miss it because if we look away for one moment we could. Then he showed on the screen projector a portrait of Jesus that a young artist painted. I almost fell out of my seat. That portrait was the exact picture of the man who kept visiting me with bright green piercing eyes! I had never seen Jesus painted this way before. I'd always imagined more of a stern Jesus liked the one pictured on "The Last Supper" painting on the wall at my grandma's house. After I had the revelation, I immediately went into another vision and saw Jesus and me climbing a mountain together. I heard him say to me, *That is it. You're finally at the top of the mountain ready to soar with me.*

After church, we went to a friend's new home to bless and pray over it. In two of the rooms, she had the same portrait of Jesus that was shown on the big screen at church. Not only does God speak through people, pictures, and other things, but he confirms and reveals himself over and over again so that we can begin to grasp his nature and how good he really is.

During the next few days, the Lord had me focus on the Beatitudes, Luke 4:18, and Matthew 5:14. Jesus spoke to me through the scriptures. I heard him say, "I am expanding your borders, limits, and territories. I am taking you to a new place, and into new land, so claim it."

There was one more week until I left for Scotland. God taught me how to manage my time and how to steward every minute according to his leading and complete the things that needed to be done in his timing and order. He also multiplied my time. I wanted to enjoy the last week of being in my apartment with such great memories and friendships. It was all bittersweet. I praised him in the midst of the grey areas and just said, *God, I have no idea what you're doing and what this looks like, but I trust that you are good and you are who you say you are. I don't need to fear the future because you will be there just like you are here with me now. I thank you for your peace that surpasses all understanding and that I can do all things through Christ who strengthens me. I love you, Lord. Thank you for providing everything that I need and wonderful people to journey with me. Your provision is indescribable.*

I had three more nights in my own place. My bags were packed, and I was finishing some last-minute cleaning. I raised the remaining funds that I needed for the trip. I was even preparing my house for the guy who was moving in, believing he would encounter and come to know the Lord. I received a lot of prayer from my church fellowship and prophetic words about the clear path. The young adults pastor prayed over my feet and declared Isaiah 52:7. He encouraged me to write down my journey because he saw a typewriter with me writing. I stewarded that prophetic word and have journaled this entire journey to be able to share with you today.

Upon my return, the only plan I had was to come back to Fort Worth after Harvest School and then visit my family in Ohio. I believed the Lord would speak to me while I was gone and make the next steps really clear. I was proud of myself when I looked around and realized that I had gotten everything done and I thanked God that he was there for me each step of the way. I only did it with his help and his grace. I was in awestruck wonder that he is the waymaker and always provides for his children.

On my last night, I stood in my doorway and wept. I heard the Lord say, "You were made for this, you are ready." I looked around and noticed that my apartment didn't seem like mine anymore. The same way I felt when I left Harlingen to move here. Looking back just two months before, I thought there was no way that I could do this mission trip. I had no clue how I was going to raise $10,000, leave my apartment, read so many books, pack, leave my job, get shots, and buy all of the gear that I needed for this trip. There was no way possible. Yet God had made the impossible possible. He held my hand every step of the way.

Chapter 4

THE ARRIVAL IN SCOTLAND
"We'll see what we've never seen before"

When I arrived at the Dallas Fort Worth Airport on Friday, May 31, my travel buddy was not there yet. Due to certain circumstances, she almost missed our flight. But thankfully, we finally met up and 11 hours later, we arrived in Glasgow, Scotland. We met some of our other classmates at the airport, and I exchanged American currency for the first time for pounds. We had coffee together at a local café and got to know each other. Then we took an Uber van to the place we would be staying.

I felt like I had just touched down in New York City. People were walking everywhere and there was a lot happening on every street corner. We were all very excited to be there. When we arrived at the hostel where we would be staying the next two weeks, I was blown away by the fist-pumping techno music and the smell of stale cigarettes streaming from outside of the building. Once inside, the hostel reminded me of the club scene when I was a bartender. I recalled when my pastor talked about preparing yourself for the atmospheres in which you are getting ready to enter. He shared that if he was going to be in a night club doing ministry in Brazil, he would first listen to some of the music that he would most likely hear there to teach himself how to pray in the Spirit and stand under those circumstances.

We lined up in the main room to get our room assignments and were told who our house parents would be. I met my housemates and they were full of anticipation. We were eight girls from eight different places and from all over the world. We were divided into two rooms. Our house mom, Esther, was assigned to my room with the two other ladies for the duration of the trip. The other four that were part of our house group stayed in the room down the hall.

There were 103 students from over 20 different nations. The youngest girl was 18 and the oldest woman was in her 70s. We had four married couples; two of the couples also had a child with them. The family leading the school had two young children. There were a lot more women than men. Since this was a traveling school, we were going to spend our first two weeks in Scotland. I had prayed for months about the people that God was going to connect me with and the groups that I would be part of.

The church we were partnering with during our time in Scotland was called Ruchazie. It was a local church plant that was placed in the middle of a neighborhood full of single parent homes and lower income level families. There was a local prison nearby where many of the fathers had been sent away. Many people in the region were very much into psychics, witchcraft and astrology.

On our first night we took a bus from the hostel to Ruchazie, where we worshiped as a community. The worship was anointed and filled with the purity of God. The staff had asked the leaders that were helping with the school to stand up front by the stage. Most of them were Harvest School alumni that were now serving in Scotland. Then the students were asked to head to the altar in front of each leader and share what we were asking and believing God for in this season. I shared that I wanted to be open to whatever God wanted to do during my time at the school. I didn't want to think for one moment what would be next.

Daily we shared lunch and dinner together as a Harvest School family. It was fun to hear the stories and sacrifices of what it took for each student to get to Scotland. Besides getting to know the others who were part of the school, we were also beginning to connect with the locals.

Every morning at the hostel we would get up and head down to the lounge for breakfast and then get ready in our rooms for the day. We all would meet outside of the hostel and catch two different buses that would take us to the Ruchazie church. We would have morning and afternoon worship and teaching sessions, as well as intimate prayer times when the leaders would pray over us. We would eat lunch at the church and for dinner the team at Ruchazie would let us pack sandwiches to take back with us on the bus. Our directors who oversee all of the Harvest Schools are Mama Pamela and Papa Tony, and the leaders of our school were Kurt and Brooke, who brought their two young children. Mama Jackie was our Scottish mama, and there were also other missionaries who were part of Iris staff with us in Scotland at Ruchazie. Our daily teachings were on identity, purpose, love, anointing, discipleship, healing, mission life, family, and the Kingdom of God. We also learned how to cultivate the presence of God. I was learning how to remain in him and how the harvest comes when you lay down your life—abiding in him is the place where I am going to bear fruit. During the second day of worship, I felt the Lord say, *This is going to be a time of intercession and worship. There is going to be breakthrough in your family and in your friendships because of your intercession.* He began to show me that the apartment and everything I gave up was because I was not going to need any of that stuff once I returned. God was bringing me into the new and changing and healing me with an unquenchable love that I had never experienced before.

He continued to speak to my heart that it was all about his love. He gave me a better understanding of what it looked like to be walking in the finished work of the cross. He reminded me of the robe of righteousness I had in the previous vision during church and he told me that he has come for the lost and to redeem his sons and daughters. When we are clothed in his righteousness, we are no longer sinners but his children. The Holy Spirit was being poured out in this place and I could feel the fire of his presence all around us.

During one worship session, there was a love tunnel. This was like a fire tunnel with the laying on of hands. Basically, the Harvest School staff and others they've entrusted and who are equipped to pray, gathered around making two parallel lines, and then we lined up in a single file line and went through this love tunnel. The leaders prayed and prophesied what they heard God speaking to us. It was like a Holy Spirit welcoming party. It was such a powerful way to start off the school and encounter the fiery love of God. We didn't waste any time. I'm thankful for a company of people who step out and into the gifts of Holy Spirit and aren't afraid to be bold.

Personally, God was taking me into a hidden season where I was unseen by man so that he could clean things out of me that existed deep within my heart. It was a time where I wasn't getting approval from the world, but I was being affirmed and approved by him. This was really difficult for me. If you take over 100 people from many nations and age ranges from 18-75, you will most definitely experience challenges and things will come up, and that is where the pressing and stretching begins. It wasn't like I was around my comfortable group of friends in Texas who knew me and my heart or around my church family who constantly encouraged and affirmed me. Here, I was only connecting with a few people and it seemed different than what I anticipated. I thought I would be making friends instantly, connecting and going deep with a mission-minded community. Instead, God immediately began taking us corporately to such a deep place of healing that we were all like fish out of water.

I was struggling with feeling unnoticed during our morning gatherings of worship. I was not the one who was being encouraged or touched like I had previously experienced. During worship, I would have my hands raised and see the leaders going up and down each aisle praying over each student, but for some reason they would just pass by me. It was unintentional, but the enemy was using this to draw up distraction and confusion in my heart. God was so graciously exposing the hurt in my heart from past rejection. *Did God even see me and was he even there? Why wouldn't the leaders simply make a straight line and pray for everyone?* When I saw people being left out, I always wanted to advocate for them. But now, it was happening to me.

I had previously experienced many God-encounters, including through several well-known evangelists and leaders in the Body of Christ, so I wasn't sure where these feelings of rejection were coming from. I could feel myself reverting back to old behaviors and orphan mindsets of running away, putting walls up, and isolating myself to feel protected. God wanted to remove these ways of thinking and the walls that I had put up, so that I could experience his complete healing and freedom from this mindset.

One morning as I was struggling with this, I suddenly remembered what our Scottish leader, Mama Jackie, had taught us on day two of the school: *I actually don't need to do anything besides remember who I am in him, and where I come from which is heaven. I am a daughter of the highest God.* All of a sudden, a woman leader came over and touched me. I just began to cry and felt the Lord's presence over me. I immediately felt loved by him. Our class worshiped and cried out for revival as the Body of Christ. The fire fell on each one of us as we lay on the ground and surrendered to him.

Through it all, God began to show me the things that I needed to start releasing to him and that it was okay to be in a season of feeling unwanted because he was turning around the lies and using it for good; it was never his truth or his desire for me. This was a time of protection and a shadowing under his wing.

The spirit of comparison was also beginning to creep in as I noticed I was comparing myself to others, such as those getting more attention or if someone was prettier than me or was more liked by other people. It always amazes me how God can use familiar situations to get really deep into our hearts and pull out things that he wants to heal. The enemy loves to torment us, but God cares so much about our hearts being purified and being completely in love with him. He wants us to love and see people the way he sees them. He doesn't want anything to hinder that growth or love that he died for us to have.

Whenever I began to feel neglected, everything in me wanted to run away and be done. But let's face it, in mission school there's nowhere to run. You're constantly surrounded by people everywhere you go. I recognized that I needed to get healing from this and be free once and for all. I only needed to remember who I was and whose I was.

Chapter 5

THE TRUTH OF GOD'S LOVE

We had been in Scotland for about a week, and our school was getting ready to break off into their scheduled outreach groups to travel throughout the United Kingdom for a couple of days. Iris had sent an email prior to beginning the school inviting us to participate in an outreach throughout the UK during our time in Scotland. We could choose between about 11 sites. The places ranged from England, Wales, Poland, Sweden, and many more. We could also stay at Ruchazie. I decided to choose Ruchazie Church, there in Scotland, to do my outreach. I felt the Lord tell me that there was a blessing in staying. I asked the Lord what his heart for the people of Ruchazie was and heard that he wanted them to know truth. They needed to know the testimony of Jesus.

Everyone took off the next day except for the Ruchazie team. They traveled by bus, car, and plane to their designated outreaches.

The anthem for our school was "We believe we'll see what we've never seen before." We were declaring every day through song and prophecy that we were going to see a new move of God during our time and season there.

On the first day of our outreach, we walked to the bus stop with our Ruchazie outreach group and headed over to the church. Our mission was to plow the garden and get rid of all the weeds so that the church could plant new crops. Some were assigned to work with the children inside and others were picking up trash around the neighborhood. This was hard work! I didn't know the first thing about gardening and how to get these tools to work the way we wanted them to.

As we worked together, our group began to bond, share stories, and help each other get the garden looking nice. Everyone had such a servant heart, and I knew that the time we were sowing into this area was going to bear much fruit. I got to connect with a woman who served in many roles at the church and hear her testimony about how she led her family to faith. I also encountered a girl who shared about reincarnation and things that she believed in. I realized that in this area there was a lot of witchcraft as well as different belief systems that had bound people in confusion. Psychics and connecting with the dead were a commonality. This tied back to the word that God had given me about the people coming to know the Word and truth that Jesus is the way, the truth, and the life.

We were planning to have a huge gala that weekend called The Source. The leader of the Source, Heather, who had trained under John Paul Jackson, was coordinating the event. We gathered the outreach team together for a meeting the night before and had dinner, prayed, and Heather assigned everyone to the station they would be tending at the gala. The stations included the kid's area, prophetic painting/art, dream interpretation and cleaning up the neighborhood. The mission behind the gala was to share the Gospel, love on the people, gather the community together, and see Jesus encounter and touch their hearts. Heather paired me with her as the dream interpretation team. She and I sat side by side with a table in front of us and people who were interested in having their dreams interpreted would take their turn and come and sit with us. It was an honor to be part of this prayer team and to hear the people of Ruchazie share about their dreams and encounters in the spiritual realm. I got prophetic pictures for a couple of the people and God crashed into their hearts as I released what he was showing me. I saw an older man we ministered to as a little boy in the hay fields and saw that God was taking him back to those places to heal things in his life. I prophesied over a woman as I saw her life as an emerging highway that went in a lot of different directions. She was in the fast lane. God wanted to give her peace and was leading her on his narrow pathway. She confirmed specific details about the highway and had such an excitement to follow Jesus on his way. Heather taught me and helped me discern which dreams were from God and which ones weren't. She said the dreams that were not from God typically were the ones in black and white and also included dreams where they are trying to bring loved ones back from the dead. We finished the evening sharing testimonies with one another. We shared stories of how God used each of us to bless the people and the children. It brought so much joy to our hearts.

All of my roommates had left for different parts of the United Kingdom, so I was going to be home alone for a few days. I didn't want to be alone; I had just made some friends and now they were all gone. I was also desiring a spouse. I had heard so many romance stories about how people met their spouse at Harvest School. This was like discipline 101 to keep my eyes focused on Jesus in all things, let go of all expectations, and press into his love for me. During this time, I had to renew my mind and take every thought captive from what I was experiencing.

On Sunday, we went to White Inch Church with our Ruchazie team. The power of the Holy Spirit fell, and I was frozen in the glory. When I looked over, a lady named Lorna was next to me. At the end of service, Lorna shared that she suffered from illness and it had kept her from doing things that she once enjoyed. She was in a lot of pain. I prayed with Lorna that morning and am believing that she is healed and whole today. God's positioning and placing people in our path is always for his timing and purposes to bring his glory.

We took a bus after White Inch to a Scottish museum and danced and hung out. We then headed back to Ruchazie that evening to cook dinner in their kitchen for the Sunday night service. I had never ridden in a European car and been on the opposite side of the road before. It was quite an experience. That evening, our team led the church service with testimonies and a message preached by one of our students. Members of our team shared how they came to know the Lord and how Jesus transformed them. One had been delivered from a heroin addiction; others had a horrible family life growing up with abusive parents. Each story was unique and powerful and spoke of how God transforms. God was getting all of the glory for our stories and the people of Ruchazie were touched.

We all gathered together as a full class the next day for worship and teaching. Everyone was back from their extended outreaches and shared with the class about the powerful times they had experienced and the places they visited. Some stayed with families, some visited the Auschwitz concentration camp in Poland, and others attended a conference.

I asked the Lord what his expectations were regarding what he wanted me to receive from Harvest School, and I strongly felt it was restoration in my life. This meant deliverance from everything that was not from him, and also coming to the end of my selfish ways that were not of him. I asked what the plan was to see those expectations met and I felt it was to posture my heart to be open to whatever he wanted to do. The next day, I felt the Lord tell me to buy a ring because I was engaged to him; this would be a reminder every day of his love for me.

One of the last days in Scotland, the Lord gave me a specific encounter, fulfilling the word restoration he had spoken over me. During worship I went into a vision and I was lying down with Jesus. He was erasing all shame and making me pure again. He was washing away abuse and bad things that had happened to me. Then I saw myself out in a garden in my grandpa's backyard when I was a little girl. I had on brown overalls that hung low and were huge on me. I was so weighed down. I began to take each leg out of the overalls, and I saw chains being broken off of me. I saw the weight I had been carrying around of dirt and disgust everywhere I went. As I stepped out of the overalls, I stepped into freedom and pain was erased. The purity of Jesus rose from my spirit as I wept before the Lord. Then I heard God say, "This is why I told you to wear green today because you are stepping into the new. I have made you new, and new things are coming forth. They are springing up like a garden full of freshness and light and life." There was a childlike renewal that washed over me as the overalls were stripped away. The baggage was finally gone. I no longer had to walk in shame and doubt. Jesus revealed what I look like to the Father and how he sees me as pure and holy. Thank you, Jesus. The more that I pressed into his heart, the more he continued to reveal himself to me.

The Lord gave me this song to declare unto him:

You are the truth
You are life
You are more to me
You are everything

You set us free
You are the way
The only way
It's you, Jesus, It's you, Jesus
We hunger and thirst for more of you, Jesus

Jesus, pour out your Spirit, we want more of you
Come, Holy Spirit, we want all of you
Let your fire fall, come with it all
Oh, Jesus, we just want you—we want all of you
Pierce our hearts for what pierces yours
Take our life, for we want all of you
No matter the cost
No matter the call
Come, Holy Spirit—just let your fire fall.

The Lord told me that once I realized he was more than enough for me; he would be all that I needed. I saw a picture of a cup overflowing and then I saw a picture of Jesus robed in all his royalty on a red carpet. There were jewels everywhere; we were walking down the red carpet and I was waving at people. I was very content and knew that I had all that I needed because I was with Jesus. He was everything and I was secure in him. I had no lack in my life and there was no complaining. I didn't have to worry about money because I was with the King of kings. I was royalty in him and needed nothing else because he was more than enough. I saw so much light in this vision and the heavens opened up, allowing me to experience his great love.

On that day during worship, June 13, 2019, I was washed clean again as a daughter into the righteousness of Christ. I had never stopped following him or turned my back, but this was a precious time where he was birthing and recreating new things that could only come through a purification process of my body, soul, and spirit to be seated with him in heavenly places. During worship, he began to show me that he can be trusted with who he says he is. When I believe that he truly is who he says he is, then I allow myself to receive his grace in my life.

Scotland was a sweet time of loving people and connecting with students from all over the world. The Lord confirmed many of the visions that I had before attending, including those regarding the robe of righteousness, the wedding, the setting apart—as the worship team would prophesy this as they sang. He confirmed that there was blessing in staying at Ruchazie for the outreach, as we began to grow closer with the people in the community there.

The prayer and declarations that Mama Pamela prayed were so powerful and brought healing and repentance. I had a vision during the time of ministry when she prayed about my trust issues growing up.

I know that God does not change his mind and that when he says he is going to do something that he can be trusted. I am healed by the revelation of knowing who God is and that he is my Father in heaven who keeps his word and promises. He is love and has brought me to this place to be so deeply loved by him and to experience a part of him that I had never known before. I am loved because I was created in the image of God, and I am healed of deeply rooted pain and condemnation that has now been brought to light and redeemed by the blood of Jesus.

The same way we dug and tilled the roots in the garden at Ruchazie is the same way that the Lord was supernaturally doing his work inside of me; he planted me on his soil and in his garden to bloom and bear fruit. *Who the Son sets free is free indeed. The beautiful seed has been planted to bring forth a harvest that will last a lifetime with fruit that continually bears for generations to come. The harvest is now, the harvest is ripe, and it confirmed the word of the Lord is for the seasons to come. Double harvest, double portion, double anointing. God can take the smallest thing and turn it around and make it great.*

Chapter 6

THE PROMISED LAND

Our time in Scotland was over and we were now heading to Israel. I was so overwhelmed with the goodness of all the people I had met in Scotland and continually thanked God for healing and changing my heart while I was there. I couldn't wait to see what else God was going to do as the journey continued. When I asked him what his word was for the time that I would be in Israel, I heard him say FREEDOM. I asked God for a vision and if he would show me a piece of his creative heart. I wanted to know more about my calling in life and what he had created for me to do. I asked Holy Spirit to teach me how to trust every day and to look to Jesus. What did it look like to fulfill the desires of the Spirit and not the flesh? Every day was a constant submission and surrender to his plans. The next two weeks would be a time to tangibly feel his presence and experience him in new ways through loving others.

The students were split up to travel between three different airlines to get to Israel. We all arrived in Tel Aviv, but our routes were different due to how the travel agent booked us. Everyone was feeling the weight of so much transition and moving through multiple countries in such a short amount of time. Some were battling with sickness, some were facing internal opposition, and others were sensing things in the atmosphere that were affecting their moods and wellness. I was also starting to get a little homesick and missing my family and old life. I think it's natural when you're facing change and transition to want to cling onto the familiar and comfortable and look backwards to the things that brought temporary joy and comfort. The old wineskin is comfortable. But he was doing a new thing. We began to pray prayers of protection. My team was growing closer and we were interceding and praying for one another daily.

We began in Jerusalem at the Holocaust museum called Yad Vashem. This is Israel's official memorial to the victims of the Holocaust. We walked through in small groups and were deeply moved as we realized how much people suffered and were tortured. Some of the students had also gone to Auschwitz when we did the extended outreaches and had shared their experiences with us. We took a bus to the Wailing Wall which was absolutely beautiful. The Wailing Wall is also called the Western Wall and is considered the holiest place where Jews are permitted to pray. One of the four retaining walls, the western one, is considered closest to the former Holy of Holies. The wall consists of many cracks where people fold up their prayers to God and stick them within the cracks of the wall. Everyone lines up to reach to the prayer wall. After I wrote down my prayer, I spent some time praying, then I folded up my prayer request and pressed it tightly into the deep cracks of the stone wall.

The presence of God was so tangibly strong as people cried out in deep travail.

I was honored to be able to go where Jesus walked and tour the land. Some of the places that we toured and visited were Shiloh, Ein Gedi (the largest oasis along the western shore of the Dead Sea and where David hid from Saul), Capernaum, Mount of Beatitudes, Mount of Olives, and Temple Mount. We stayed in Jerusalem, Negev, and Tiberius (Galilee). I even got to walk through Hezekiah's tunnel which is a water channel beneath the City of David. King Hezekiah had built the tunnel to prepare Jerusalem for a siege from the Assyrians. The tunnel was about a third of a mile long, and the water came up to our knees at some parts. Many students' comments were making me a bit fearful of being in the tunnel for too long and being claustrophobic because the top of the tunnel was very low. After getting to the end, I was so glad that I did it. It was a great experience. We could hear others from the team singing as they walked through, with the sounds from heaven echoing from wall to wall.

Heidi Baker met us at the Mount of Olives, which overlooks the city of Jerusalem, and we worshiped and prayed. I couldn't believe where we were. It was absolutely beautiful. The mount is known to be the place where Jesus ascended into heaven. After worship, Heidi began to pray over people and went up and down the aisles where we were standing. Later in the week, we went to the Mount of Beatitudes where she shared a teaching from the Sermon on the Mount. We were astonished by her humility and gratitude to glorify God in every situation and the intimacy that she carries with Jesus.

The more time that I got to spend with Jesus, the more the atmospheres and situations shifted. It was difficult in between classes and all of the places we were traveling, to have daily quiet time with him.

I felt him rejoicing and thanking me for coming to visit his home in Israel and making a way to be there. In the midst of the many wonderful experiences, I was still struggling with feelings of rejection, abandonment, not feeling good enough, comparison, judgement and insecurity. I could not figure out where this was coming from. I asked Holy Spirit if there was a lie that I had come into agreement with and when these feelings had started in my life. I prayed and broke off all confusion and imagination of not feeling liked or seen by others, and I released myself from all negative thoughts. I began to declare, "I am more than enough. I am seen. I am loved." I asked God what he was trying to show me through this experience. How could I receive healing and breakthrough so that I could stop trying to validate myself by showing off or striving to do or be someone that I was not? I was going to a new place in my identity within Jesus. *How can I be me and be completely loved by you?* I asked. He wanted to show me his heart for the people of Israel. In this place of his great love, I could see myself the way he sees me in his image.

We continued to tour the land by bus every morning and would get back before dark. We were assigned to three different teams and had three separate buses and tour guides. We were paired with our outreach group and a few additional groups on each bus. Because our school was so large with over 100 students, we couldn't all show up at the holy sites at once. We had to take turns. I used to have terrible motion sickness and I was afraid I would have to medicate on the trip and then miss out on the tour. God gave me supernatural strength to endure these long bus rides on curvy, mountainous hills, and healed me not only of motion sickness but also of the fear behind it.

Our Harvest 30 team went to Jerusalem House of Prayer for all Nations (JHOPAN) on the Mount of Olives and gathered to worship and pray. JHOPAN was founded by Tom and Kate Hess in 1987 and is a 24-hour house of prayer to pray for peace in Jerusalem and God's purpose in Israel and in the nations. We worshiped inside and outside the mount and prayed for the pastors. God gave us words to speak and pray over the leaders to release the joy of the Lord and bless and honor them. We spent the day blessing Israel and allowing the Lord to speak through us and pour out his Spirit.

Later that evening, I prayed for the daughter of a friend who was in my house group. She shared about the struggles her daughter faced, which were similar to what I used to deal with when it came to anxiety, phobias, fear, and worry. I couldn't believe how much our stories correlated with one another. I was thankful to be able to share the testimony of Jesus and how I was delivered with a mom who was deeply hurting and crying out for freedom for her daughter.

The next morning when I woke up, there was a gigantic, deadly looking spider in our bathroom. I am typically not scared of spiders whatsoever, but this thing was bigger than a tarantula. It was scary! We quickly used the bathroom for the essentials and got out as quickly as we could. The four of us were rushing to get ready because we were moving out again to stay at another place. We stayed at four different places in the two weeks in Israel so there was a lot of movement and transition.

We walked to breakfast from the kibbutz that we were staying at which is like a motel accommodation with many units and entries for housing. They are a unique Israeli form of hospitality. The breakfast hall was located behind the kibbutz down a trail with many left and right turns which we didn't really pay any attention to on our way there. When Monica and I arrived, they had provided a huge continental breakfast buffet for the students, but we barely had any time to eat and needed to get back to the buses and load up our luggage. We were trying to find our way back and somehow got very lost as every trail was starting to look identical. We would head one way for a while and realize that nothing looked familiar. Then we would take off and start going the other way and finally admitted that we had no idea where we were. No one spoke English. I started to feel fearful and lost in this unknown land along with the pressure to get on the buses to leave. After about 15 minutes, we found a woman who spoke English who gave us some directions and we were finally able to get our bearings and saw where we were staying. Everyone was rushing around. I got to the room and was hauling a huge bag on my back and dragging my suitcase, ready to cry because at this point, I wanted to quit and give up. Then, to top it off, I couldn't find my cell phone anywhere and my leader suggested that I go back to the breakfast hall to look for it. After just waking up to total fear of getting bit by this spider, circling around lost in the middle of nowhere where no one spoke English, and hauling my luggage, now I had to go back to the diner? I didn't think so. I started crying and began to panic as all of the stress put me over the edge. In spite of all the healing that I had experienced in my walk with the Lord, this situation triggered familiar feelings of danger and panic from past seasons of my life when I suffered with anxiety and fear.

I finally found my phone at the bottom of my purse and was able to calm down as the leader prayed for me. God was really healing me of control and giving me insight into where these deeply rooted feelings of fear and uncertainty were coming from.

Later that day, we arrived in the desert where Heidi was coming to speak. Something was not feeling right with my stomach. Holy Spirit gave me revelation that Satan was trying to target me for praying for my friend and her daughter the night before and he wanted to surround me with the familiar spirit of fear and panic that I used to experience. I felt so sick when Mama Heidi began to teach that I couldn't even sit there to listen. Other people were also really sick with the flu, so I wasn't sure what was going on. I told Mama Jackie and a couple of the other leaders that I wasn't feeling well and mentioned that I felt I was under a spiritual attack. The second that I started getting prayer, I bent forward and I could feel the heaviness and the sickness lift off of me. My body went from being completely bent forward to straight. Thank God for his revelation and deliverance. God was teaching me about the authority that I have in Jesus to push back darkness and to claim his freedom over every situation.

There were so many amazing experiences we had in Israel. I was loving my house group. We were from many different countries and places: Australia, Scotland, Leeds, England, Alabama, Canada, Texas, California. There was so much love and laughter in this group. We rotated between the eight of us when we would stay different places and we came to really enjoy and get to know one another. It was all about connection with him and connection with others. He loved each of us individually and as the family of Christ.

We continued to travel throughout the land and even stayed with the Bedouin people in the Judean desert. They shared their coffee with us, music, and many stories. We ate delicious family style meals—all of the food in Israel is absolutely delightful. There were all kinds of meats like chicken, beef, lamb, seafood, hummus dips, pita breads, salads and fresh herbs, dates, and halva, a tahini-based sweet which became my favorite dessert. We slept outside under canopy tents and camped out for the night at the village. The girls stayed on one side of the camp and the guys on the other. Heidi also came, and we went on a camel ride throughout the desert hill.

We traveled to the Dead Sea and experienced the ocean of salt and the oils of the earth. The water felt warm and oily, and it is known for its healing properties. You couldn't stay in the water too long or you could dehydrate. The buoyance was fun to experience; you would just float. After the Dead Sea, we went to the Jordan River where we had the opportunity to get baptized. Even though I was water baptized after I gave my life to Jesus, I decided to say yes to this as part of the renewal. My house mom and leader Kurt from the school baptized me while they sang and chanted, "We are the wild ones." It was glorious!

Later, we went on to the Sea of Galilee where we had a time of worship. We were split up on two boats but tied together as one team. It was breathtaking. I could hardly believe that this is the water that Jesus walked on and here we were, riding on a boat, worshiping him with the entire school.

I was beginning to see how much God was coming through and helping me with each transition from place to place and my conversations with others. He was showing me that his grace is sufficient. During worship later that night, I felt the Holy Spirit come and rest on me when one of the leaders prayed for me. Then, when the worship ended, I literally felt the lifting of his presence. To encounter him is to know him. I could feel myself walking in the love and freedom that only he can give. I woke up the next morning with the word *Elohim* in my spirit. It means THE LIVING GOD.

Chapter 7

THE COMMISSIONING

God was enlarging my capacity to receive more from the heavenly realm with him and was speaking to me in many different ways. He answered the prayers that I had been praying to know more specifically about his call for my life. He revealed them on the day of our "Great Commissioning from Israel." He showed me pictures of my destiny and who he had predestined me to become. This was much bigger than my plan of wanting to know what profession I was called to or "who" I was going to be. That is what the world teaches us. Instead, God was revealing to me his heart for my lifelong call and how to abide in a continual process of trust.

In our Monday morning session, the Lord took me into a vision where I saw a cave. It looked like an igloo, and there was a door on the front of it. I knocked on the door of the cave and Jesus answered and let me in. I went to sit at a small, round table with him and we began to have coffee together. As we sat together, I looked around the room inside the cave and there were people lined up all around the walls side by side. They looked like aliens or skeletons but somehow, I knew that they were people. There were dry bones all around, with empty and lost souls. As Jesus and I talked, I felt the impression that I was to speak life into these skeletons that had no function in their dry bones.

As I began to call forth the people that were lined up around the cave, I felt an urgency and command from the Lord to speak life to them. When I began to speak to the dry bones, I saw their bodies fill with life again and they began to move into their identity and calling. I heard in my spirit, multi-generational ministry. I saw women begin cleaning and dancing all around, and I saw people that were stagnant and lost coming alive and stepping into who they were created to be with joy and laughter. I believe this was a commissioning and confirmation of my call to evangelism, discipleship, and mothering the orphans.

I knew that God was speaking to me about the call that is on my life to bring people into the kingdom and equip them to see their destiny fulfilled. God was revealing parts of his heart. He loves it when we partner with him and catch his vision for the lost and the ones he died for. He makes beauty from ashes for his sons and daughters to have life. He has given us authority to speak life into dry bones and make them come alive.

He then gave me the word *trust*. I saw him untying the boat—which I believe represented my comfort zone—that I would often see in my visions and that was always close to the shore. Adrienne, the worship leader, began to sing about the Father dancing with us, which was also confirmation of previous visions. I placed my feet upon his as he directed and guided me into this beautiful dance of life with him. Jesus was dancing all around. As I sang and worshiped, the power of God hit me so hard that I started to feel my body bend down and my knees sank lower and lower until my heart was burning and beating very fast; the love of God brought me to tears.

Today was also the Great Commissioning out of Galilee for our Harvest School 30 with Heidi Baker. The ceremony represented when Jesus commissioned his disciples out of Galilee. We had a fire tunnel which was similar to the love tunnel in Scotland. Harvest School 30 was really significant to all of us because at age 30 Jesus' ministry began. As I went through the tunnel and the team began to pray and prophesy over me, I heard the Lord speak to me about Los Angeles and India. He spoke to me about both of these places like a heavenly download in the vision as I went through the tunnel. The fire of God came, and I landed in the back of the room with my left arm shaking and my whole body on the ground kneeled over receiving all that Holy Spirit had for me. I heard the Lord say that he was calling me not only to the poor, but to the rich and poor in spirit. The commissioning that came out the fire tunnel birthed something in my heart for the lost and to do the work of the Lord that he was preparing for me.

That afternoon, Heidi spoke from Ephesians, "What does it mean to be a son?" She shared about us being adopted into sonship and how we are no longer orphans. She referred to the analogy that orphans will go to a buffet and take so much because they don't realize that they can go back for more and that there is always enough. There is no lack in the Kingdom of God, she reassured us.

In the evening, a guest speaker came and taught. He said that the most neglected mission field is Jesus's heart. We are created to minister to God first and then to people. He shared how God wants our fellowship before anything else. It is commendable how obedient Abraham was when he heard the call from God on his life. He went out the next day to fulfill it. "When we understand God's heart for his son and Israel," he said, "everything will shift and be different." He continued, "There is no one more misunderstood and abused than God." *God, give us a heart for what breaks yours. Let us minister to you God from a place of your love and desire to please you that flows out of our hearts. Lord, we repent for making it about us. We turn our hearts back to you and say yes to the call that you have on our lives. Let us walk in complete obedience to your story that you have written about us and to have boldness and grace to carry out the call that you have spoken to each one of us. In your name we pray. Amen.*

This truly was a season of being hidden under his wing, protection, consecration, and being set apart. That night, as we went into worship, Adrienne prophetically sang and led from such a place of his presence that there were heavenly encounters of gladness and mercy from the throne room of grace. I felt I was to get down on the ground in a ball, almost like I did during a tornado drill back in grade school, and as soon as I did, I heard the Lord say, *I am your safe place.* Then I felt the heavy, glorious presence and peace of God. I lay down on my face and heard him saying, *I am hiding you right now.* I wasn't sure what this meant. It was supernatural and I was in another realm. Psalm 91 immediately came to my mind. He was hiding and protecting me. As I soaked in his presence, his weighty glory was pressing me down on the ground into this awkward position in front of all of my peers.

When you are overcome by the Holy Spirit, your mind is still capable of thinking and forming thoughts, but you physically cannot move, nor do you want to move because he is downloading such heavenly particles of the divinity and nature of Jesus. The healing and downloads from heaven are so vivid and comforting that you cannot help but want to stay in that moment with him forever. The whole time the speaker preached, I just stayed on the ground in front of the class and one of my kind friends covered me with her scarf. The man speaking, an evangelist and Messianic Jew, was sharing about reconciliation between the Arabs and Jewish people in the inner city through intercession in the streets and bringing groups together for creative ideas and purposes.

I wanted to get up so that I wasn't just "slain in the Spirit" in front of the entire class, but God was saying that he was hiding me for this time and that he would release me when he was ready. Then I saw pictures of Heidi in the dirt and he said, *That is going to be you; you are going to be in the dirt loving my people.* I would try to lift my elbow, but I just could not move so I stayed on the floor twisted up in some uncomfortable position. At some point I asked God, *Can I please get up yet?* I felt in that moment that my life is going to look like a representation of what I looked like right then, with my face in the dirt waiting on him and being under his covering. I heard him say, *I am transforming your heart and setting you apart.* My heart and breathing became really heavy as I began to join in with him and allow him to transform my heart. Then I was finally able to pick myself off of the ground, and I sat up on the floor. The glory was still so heavy that I wanted to fall flat on my face but instead my whole body began to shake; I couldn't even open my eyes to look at the man speaking. It was really hard for me to sit there in front of everyone because now I was just spinning and a bit uncomfortable as my body just shook throughout the rest of the message. I sat there and continued to receive. I felt the anointing this man carried was the same impartation that the Lord was giving me to evangelize and bring reconciliation and hope to people.

The next morning, I was riding the bus to one of our sites and as I gazed out of the window, I had such a revelation of God the Father, Jesus my beloved, and Holy Spirit my comforter, just wrapping their arms of protection around me. I felt really safe and loved and for once I knew that I was going to be okay; that they were not going to let anything happen to me. I felt that I had protective and comforting parents watching over me. There was such a remarkable grace and a release from needing to protect myself—a defense mechanism that I had developed in the past—and I knew that God was my defender.

I was receiving so much revelation. When I would go back to my room, I would begin to process with him and write down what he was saying. I received immense healing from my community of sisters in the faith through sharing my heart with them and our pouring into one another.

During our outreach in Galilee, we partnered with a local nonprofit called the Beautiful Land Initiative and picked up trash. It blew my mind how careless some people could be by throwing furniture and other trash and debris into the beautiful ocean and land in Israel. During this team gathering, the Lord showed me to bless others in the moments where they are excelling and shining. In my flesh, I tend to get really annoyed with people when I don't agree with their motives, but the more grace that I let flow from me, the more that I was able to exchange God's grace instead of judgment. I was so used to standing out and being a leader, but in this hidden season, God was teaching me to stand back while others shine. I learned humility.

My heart was beginning to burn day by day with the desire for inner city missions. I kept hearing Hollywood and Iris inner city. How was this going to connect? Brooke and Kurt, the leaders of Harvest School, have an inner-city prayer ministry in St. Louis. They were going to be gathering students and sharing more about this as the days went on. I wanted to learn more and find out what God was saying about this.

One evening, the eight of us in my house group gathered and prayed. My best friend, Monica, who I met during this trip, started praying about going low so that she could lift others high. It was the most beautiful prayer and the presence of God was on it strongly. God brought back to my memory that I had asked him to send a strong friend to help me on this trip. I mostly meant physically strong, which Monica was, but he gave me such a sister in the Lord. We fit so perfectly together, and God had arranged and ordained it all. Out of the 103 students, he picked a perfect match that I would do life with and we would sharpen one another. I was so undone by his goodness in that moment and I felt the Lord saying to me, "Just like I picked Monica to be your best friend, so I will also pick for you the best husband that matches you and fits you perfectly." I continued to cry at his goodness and that even this friendship was going to teach me how to steward, bless, and love well. Through it, I would learn a lot about giving and taking, loving and receiving, and walking in humility. I felt this friendship would also teach me how to love and honor my husband and how to share and submit everything that the Lord has given me. I was praising and thanking God for her.

One of the challenges of traveling was entering into the different spiritual atmospheres; perceiving the generational strongholds over the land and experiencing a heightened awareness and discerning of spirits. There were times when my moods would fluctuate greatly, and thoughts were not mine. During this time, I was reminded to take every thought captive and hold it to the Word of God. If it didn't match his character and what he says about me, then it couldn't be from him. The best way that I discern whether it's God who wants to reveal something to my heart or whether Satan wants to throw me off course is if God is giving me revelation in love. Does the outcome represent the nature and character of Christ?

There was a battle going on in the spirit in Israel, and darkness was being revealed. Satan was using things from students' past to bring confusion and division, so we stood in the gap and prayed. God is peace. I knew that there was great impact in the circle of my roomies, and that God was doing such a magnificent work in our hearts.

We were wrapping up our time in Israel and were about to move on to Madagascar. I inquired of the Lord what he had for the people there. I journaled and sought his face because I wanted to know his heart for the Malagasy people. I asked him, "Lord, what do you want to show me about Madagascar?" I heard him say, *I want to show you my love for the people.* "Lord, how can I pray for them?" *Pray that they would find their identity in me.* "How can I pray for the school?" *Pray and break off selfishness and turn it into selflessness.* "What do you want to show me through this experience?" *I want to show you that you can do all things through Christ Jesus who strengthens you.* God encouraged me to persevere and continue to run the race with him.

Chapter 8

THE GOD OF THE BREAKTHROUGH

We made it to Madagascar after a 24-hour flight with a layover in Johannesburg. It was quite the adventure and fun to travel with the students. I had a hard time leaving Israel because of all of the splendor and beauty and closeness that I had felt with Jesus there. He had given me so much revelation. I also loved the delicious Mediterranean food and the warm, hot sun. I converted my money at the airport and received the Malagasy Ariary (MGA). Even my mathematical skills were growing from the UK, Israel, and now Malagasy money conversion.

As soon as we got off of the plane, they had us put all of our luggage and belongings on top of a random van, and then we got into another van where we were piled deep on top of one another while we just left our stuff with strangers. This did not sit well with me. I mean, I was going to be here for a month and if somehow my suitcase fell off of the van or these guys decided to just take our stuff and sell it, what in the heck would I do for the next month? I had to trust God in this moment—when everyone else seemed excited and were joyfully shouting despite being so crowded, I was silent, confused, and completely overwhelmed.

We arrived at the Christian facility where, for the next month, we would eat, sleep, go on outreaches, and have our teachings for the school each day. The building was brown brick, a few stories high, and in the middle of all-dirt surroundings. This building housed all of the women and families. There was a children's school behind that was not Iris-affiliated but a private school for elementary kids. There was another building up the hill with the kitchen area to eat and dine. The guys had their own building on the same campus. The room I was assigned to was on the first floor and closest to the outside. As soon as we walked into the tiny room, I saw a set of bunk beds and two single beds. It smelled of wet mold, and it was freezing. There was a rug covering the dirt floor. A single lightbulb provided white and bright light, making me think of jail cell living and definitely not a homey environment. The smell of the trash pile burning outside was intense and since our room was at the end of the hall by the door, the smell blew right into our bedroom. The doors did not lock and were left open at all hours of the night. Our bedroom window faced the playground where the kids played basketball loudly throughout the day.

I said to my roommates, "I cannot stay in this room. I am super allergic to mold, and my allergies will make me so sick if I stay here. I just can't. My pillow and bed linens are stained and seem unwashed.

And we have nowhere to put our stuff." Even though it was now July, it was winter in Madagascar and it became dark around 5:00 p.m. This was where I was challenged the most in regard to my comfort zone and life as I knew it. To be honest, my skin was crawling within a short time after arrival. I didn't even know what to think. I thrive in organization, structure, and cleanliness. Mission life is often the opposite of this. Israel's living conditions weren't ideal in every circumstance, but at least we had hot water—something else I quickly learned we would do without—and a room that didn't smell like it could possibly give me an asthma attack at any moment. And we were going to be spending the next month here. I went and found my house mom and told her that there was no way that I could stay in that room; that I was super allergic to mold. She let me know that if I needed to move rooms, someone in her room could switch with me.

However, I absolutely loved all of my sister roommates, especially my new best friend, Monica. I knew that if I switched rooms, I would no longer be with her. I knew my decision could make a difference and could possibly mess up the plan that God had for me which was to put me into that exact room on that exact bed for his purposes and to humble me. I decided to stay in the room that I was assigned to. Probably one of the hardest things for me on the field was trying to resist asking a million questions about what would happen next and to trust God's plan instead.

The toilets were also altogether different than anything I had ever experienced. I was not used to going to the bathroom without an actual seat. It was really interesting. I needed God's grace more than ever at this point. There was no way that I could live here for a month without having Jesus every second of the day. My roommates also had to pray over my bed because I was a bit freaked out. I felt really bad because I didn't want to complain, but if you've never been to another country before, let alone a third world country, and you've never done missions, you are in for quite the surprise. I had never inhaled pollution to this extreme before and had always suffered with allergies. I was completely out of my comfort zone and it was time to dig deeper into his lovingkindness and grace and put my flesh to death.

Madagascar was the place that God had been speaking to me about from the very beginning during my encounter at the evangelism school. But the photos that I had seen on Google were of beaches and greenery and this was red dirt and dust. This apparently was a different part of the region without the beautiful beaches, rainforest and blue and green bodies of ocean and trees. *Could this really be the place that the Lord has called me to and is this what it really looks like? Did I hear God correctly and was this the vision that I had of Madagascar or did I just make this up?* Questioning God and his voice was often a habit of mine when things didn't make sense or go according to my plan. Missions was looking a lot different than what I had anticipated, and I was in for a wild new ride with Holy Spirit as the navigator.

I was growing closer with my roommates and we took time to pray over our room. My body was so tense from so much newness and all the things that were going on in the atmosphere. There was such a heaviness in the spiritual realm, a spirit of apathy, and we were all realizing that God was beginning to take us even deeper than ever before. God was doing such a tremendous work in our hearts from the stretching. I couldn't even form a sentence or make a facial expression because of how intense the entire situation was for me and adjusting to the new setting, climate, and surroundings.

It was the first day of class and we were having a "Burn." A Burn is a time to worship the Lord and dance, sing, praise, create, or however you want to express yourself. It was really beautiful to see people in my class exploring new things and stepping out in new ways. As soon as I entered the room, all I could do was cry. I was so undone by all that was going on. As I sat on the ground and cried out to the Lord, I said, "I hate this God, I am dying." Everything was really new and scary to me and at the same time my heart just burned with passion for him because he is so worthy of it all. When I finally opened my eyes and wiped my face, I saw people dancing around and jumping. I could barely lift my head. Even in the deep places of self-doubt, uncomfortableness, and fear, I knew that God was with me, he saw me, and felt the pain that I was experiencing. He wanted to comfort me and didn't enjoy seeing me suffer. Glimpses of my life were passing by me of my dog that died, my apartment, my car, years of deep decisions made manifest in the life that I had chosen through the leading of the Holy Spirit, and the yeses that had brought me to this place on the dirt ground crying out to him. I wanted to run back to the comfortable places. But Jesus, who died for me, had called me out of darkness and into his glorious light to be joined with him and to stand firmly on his foundation.

I repented from a victim mentality but extended grace to myself as I allowed the Holy Spirit to comfort me and to intercede on my behalf. In my weakness, he is made strong. I declared that there is no condemnation for those who are in Christ Jesus. I would live according to the Spirit and not according to the flesh. All thoughts of insecurity and not feeling good enough had to leave. During time of prayer and intercession, God gave me a picture of Jesus sitting with me, and we began to climb the mountain together again. This brought me renewed strength. He was showing me how to be content and have joy in all circumstances.

The staff cautioned us about spending too much time and money at the local corner store, Shoprite. "It's so easy to miss what God is doing during your time there because you spend all of your time buying snacks at the store and eating your feelings, which can be a huge distraction." As time went on, I began to see what they were talking about. However, I also have a very fond memory. My first day at Shoprite, as I was cruising down the aisle, over the loudspeaker I heard the song, "We Belong Together" which is a classic from my favorite movie growing up, "La Bamba." It's about Ritchie Valens, who was a young Hispanic musician and a superstar. I couldn't believe that I was across the world and my favorite song as a child was playing. Never in a million years had I ever heard this song playing anywhere—let alone millions of miles away from home. I began to sing and spin and dance through the aisle and was so captivated by God and his goodness that I just knew deep down this sweetness could have only come from him. There were many moments like this when I felt so far away from everything, but he felt so near. I quickly began to realize that no matter where I was, he was there. The same God that had created me, had created all of these precious Malagasy people and children. He knew every hair on their head and had all of their days numbered which were far more precious than the grains of sand.

We had class every morning and evening except for when we were on outreach. We had several remarkable speakers come and teach us what they had learned on their journey of following Jesus. They taught about identity, freedom, faith, and endurance to persevere on the journey and to continue saying *yes*.

During class one day, our speaker, Tineke, led us in an exercise where we were to face our fears. She placed a chair at the front of the room, then picked it up and slammed it back down and proclaimed, "I am going to face it." We could no longer run and hide. We knew that we were going to face our fears today. She told anyone who felt led to face their fears to line up. The whole class lined up one by one and walked up to the chair and faced it, proclaimed it, picked up the chair and slammed it down and broke agreement with the fear that each one of us faced. I surrendered and laid down my desire for independence.

It was the 4th of July and we had less than a month to go before the school ended. I was back on the floor telling the Lord how hard this time was for me. It was winter and cold, and I wanted to be with my family enjoying the nice weather and surrounded by people that I loved. I heard the Lord say, "Let me lead you." Psalm 23 came to mind: "He leads me beside still waters and makes me lie down." Then I saw Jesus comforting me. *Today is a day of freedom. Freedom from self and from expectations of others. Free from my plans and surrendering myself to him.* I sat on the ground and reached my hand out to him and he lifted me up to join in worship. *The promise doesn't always look like what we think. But I know from my history with the Lord that I can trust him and that his leadership is perfect. Sometimes I have to face my doubt and be okay with my weakness. It's in this place that I can cast all of my cares on him because he cares for me.*

From the beginning of the journey, we were assigned to outreach teams who we would be grouped with throughout the school. My outreach team in Madagascar was led by Don and Jackie, powerful husband-and-wife leaders who were pastoral, loving, and filled with so much wisdom. Our team was growing closer and spending more time together at the Christian facility. We would fellowship weekly and have meetings to check in and share what God was doing in our hearts. We would also break up into even smaller groups and share parts of our story or things that we were struggling with and pray together. We were all beginning to get more comfortable in mission life of freezing cold showers, overflowed toilets, no running water, smells, washing clothes by hand in bins, and eating what was put in front of us.

There were a couple of Iris sayings that we would joke about that weren't funny in the moment. "Hurry up and wait" was one of them. "Go low and slow" is one of Heidi's favorites. I like to be quick and don't enjoy waiting. These phrases were a new concept for me. I have grown to appreciate them.

On our first Sunday in Madagascar, we were having church together. Rolland Baker, who is also the founder of Iris Global, came to visit us. The boys and girls from the children's home came that day as well. The joy of the Holy Spirit fell upon us and laughter broke out around the room. People were being touched by God as Rolland spoke about the Kingdom. A little girl who was sitting on the floor next to me kept reaching across to put her hand on my head, and each time she did, the fire of God would fill me and my cheeks got red and hot. I had to close my eyes because the glory of God was so strong. Throughout the service, I kept picturing California and thinking about what I was going to do after the school. The whole morning was filled with God's goodness and presence.

I found out later that day that the girl who kept putting her hand on my head was named Monica, and that she was deaf. The Spirit of God is no stranger to the spirit of infirmity. He continually pours out his love for his heavenly children on this earth.

Rolland would go around and touch people with the microphone and they would begin to scream and laugh and giggle hysterically. It was a beautiful picture of the Lord's contagious laughter and delight over us.

Rolland's Teaching

Rolland taught us about enjoying God and what the Kingdom of God is like. He said, "Our relationship with God is not contingent upon the doing or working for him, but it's actually about getting to know him as a companion and a Father in heaven—so what does rest in him actually look like on this earth? Do our families and others who don't have a relationship with God and know us actually think that we enjoy our time with the Father?" Rolland asked, "What does it look like to need Jesus more than you need the healing? What if God answered every prayer? We would treat God like a slave. What if he gave us every request and told us our entire lives and what it was going to be like? Would we even need to seek him anymore, or would we have it all figured out already? If God tells you to do something other than what you are doing, then do it. Be so in love with God, that it isn't about seeking out the miracles and the signs and wonders, but it's about him. If we seek first the Kingdom of God, and not prayer and worship, then we can be in love with the God who does the signs and the miracles and can be in love with people whom God has created."

Rolland's teachings brought so much revelation to my heart and imparted the fear of the Lord to really abide and know him more. It brought me back to the place where Jesus was my first love and nothing else mattered. It made me want to tell more people about him and what the Kingdom of God is like. His teaching challenged me in my priorities, prayers, goals, and really brought my heart back to the why and how I first came to know Jesus. I asked myself, *Does my journey reflect joy in my relationship with Jesus, or just going through the motions and experiencing one hardship after another?* Even though the path is narrow, I can see how the pressing, perseverance, and trusting in God has shaped my heart and has taken me from glory to glory to know him, love him, and seek him even more. I was forever changed by Rolland's wisdom and fatherly heart to lead us and come all the way to Madagascar to teach us the things that God has taught him and showed him over the years.

Will's Teaching

Will Hart taught us during the afternoon session about the fruit of our lives and what it means to step into such faith that it actually scares people. He used the term "holy violence" for when we are going after the Kingdom of God. "You cannot go after the things God has spoken over your life if you are still afraid of what people think. God wants to use each of us in life for his holy calling and the purpose he has for us. It's quite alright for our family or the world not to understand what God is doing in our lives. His calling is not going to make sense. It has to be supernatural and out of the comfort zone. The things of God are the same things that cannot be understood or considered in the natural realm and how the world operates. God is the one who put these desires in our heart when we became one with Christ. When we move forward into the things he has called us to, it is going to look like something beyond what our minds can grasp. Obedience and the yes look like something. It is the impossible that he calls us to." Will concluded, "God already has a Heidi Baker. Who is he calling you to be?"

As I reflected on Will's teaching, I realized how I didn't give up all the good things in my life because God threatened to strike me down if I didn't. I did it from a place of love and adoration in my heart to the one who is worthy of it all. He gave me every single blessing and because I love him so much, I was willing to lay everything down in order to move forward into the deep waters and the places that he was calling me to. My obedience to him was more important than letting fear and the things of the world cloud my vision and keep me stuck in a place that I knew was not my true purpose and calling. I was fully ready to tune into God's heart and see what he was speaking to me through the desires that he has placed in my heart—which are actually his desires. He gave me his heart to move forward in this season of life and he has plans that exceed any expectation that I could even think of. He is God. I didn't need to continue to question what he was asking me to do because I know that his character is good and that he is faithful according to his plan and what he has spoken.

The next day, Will preached again about stepping out of the safe territory and into the places where we aren't safe. Jesus called us to give our lives away and to not consider our lives more valuable than they are. He said, "Just go and release the Kingdom of God amongst non-believers and people who persecute you. Jesus was persecuted daily, but he remained close to the Father and continued to do what the Father was telling him to." God is the great adventurer and designer of our lives. He knows every detail, every thought, and every part of our story that tells of his great love and mercy for us.

Will also stressed that we are not to despise the small things, because it is all given by God. He already knows what's going to happen. God wants someone who can see beyond the facts and someone who will go amongst the wolves. Will told us something that changed my worldview forever. He said, "Fear is faith in Satan—it elevates the lie." He shared that everywhere the Lord took him, he was going to be fully in that place.

I pondered on my life and thought, *Isn't it funny how we want to be in a certain place and then God orchestrates and opens the doors for us to be there, but when we get there we want to be somewhere else?* The most foundational stones of Will's walk were the most uncomfortable and most unprepared places.

Will prayed for us to be free from the fear of man and for it to be broken off of our lives so that we can run freely into the things that God has. He also prayed for us that evening as we gathered around for an impartation night. There was an altar call where we could go up to the front and receive prayer. I didn't go to the front but stood up with the group of students in the middle. Will prayed for the fire of God to come and Papa Don and Jackie, my outreach team leaders, stood in front of me. Jackie grabbed my hand and imparted joy, then Don put his fingers on my forehead and began to pray. My entire body got hot like fire and I fell back laughing hysterically and was stuck on the floor once again with the weighty glory of God. I couldn't stop laughing. Jackie grabbed my hand and shouted, "Freedom!" I received the joy of the Lord and there was a lightness in my spirit. God had been speaking to me about freedom since Israel, but here in Madagascar, he released freedom directly into my spirit. I had truly been set free.

As I processed all that was taught that day, I thought about the lie that I was sometimes tempted to believe: "I gave all of this stuff away and will be left with nothing." But the truth was that it was such a beautiful exchange of my heart for his, and I came away with more joy, peace, love, and freedom than I ever had experienced before. I think about Jesus' life and how difficult it had to have been for him to go to the cross and suffer. His body was broken, and his blood was shed through a brutal crucifixion in obedience to his Father. He died so that we could live with him forever in eternity. He even died for those who he knew wouldn't choose him. This is true love.

All of my years before knowing Jesus were lived in complete fear and double-mindedness. I never knew that I had partnered with the enemy and allowed him to take over and destroy my life. It makes sense now because when I came to know Jesus, anxiety and fear were no longer a part of my identity.

Knowing Jesus has been the greatest gift and my favorite treasure of all. Sometimes the most challenging places we go will be the very building blocks that expand our feet on the rock in which we stand. His foundation never changes.

I wrote in my journal: *It's been totally worth it to me, but it hasn't come without a price. I've had to miss out on years of family life, making friends just to leave them, going places where I knew no one and starting over, and most of all, trusting God when it's looked completely impossible to pick up my cross and follow him time and time again. I'm so thankful for the community that he has placed in my life and the voices of women who encourage me, sharpen me, and speak truth. I want to follow him all of the days of my life. He has invited us to journey with him each day in this grand adventure of life. He loves the struggle because he knows that it is producing perseverance inside of us, and that it is completely impossible without him.*

Pastor Surprise's Teaching

Another speaker was Pastor Surprise Sithole, author of *Voice in the Night*, which I had read before coming to Harvest School. He is a wild Jesus follower and his stories are unreal and so powerful.

He taught on the goodness of Jesus and that all good things flow from him. He can move us on to what he has, but if our eyes become focused on that and not on him, we will face trouble. Some examples he gave were being focused on money instead of the mission. It's not about writing books, it's about Jesus. He said, "If you really love God, he will help you to love people. Very few seek for him with all of their heart. He is able to make himself known. What does it mean to search for him instead of anything else? Put everything else to the side. Blessed are you who believe and don't see. He is worth ditching everything else to find him. We need to know God better. When you go after God, he takes care of the money."

My faith was stirred to truly pursue the Lord on an even more intimate level. My excitement and love for him continued to grow when hearing the testimonies of his goodness. Everything else was stripped away, and my eyes could only see Jesus through the eyes of love. I saw how deeply he cared about every speaker, student, and person that he created.

Loving the Lord Above All

To close out the week, Rolland finished teaching about our ministry to love the Lord and to not be in love with the world. He continued to share that Jesus is our only desire and everything in our lives comes from that place. It goes back to the first commandment to love the Lord with all of your heart, soul, mind, and strength.

He said, "The real joy only comes from being in an intimate relationship with the Father. It doesn't come from what we have or who we are with. Our joy is not defined by how much money we have or how high we can climb on the success ladder. It comes from our identity in him and who he created us to be. You become a saint when Jesus is enough for you and you don't need back-up. Rejoicing in the Lord is not optional. When we are so in love with someone, all we want to do is spend time with them."

Rolland warned us to be careful what we are building because it will be judged. He said, "Build on Jesus. He is the answer to everything. The questions always will come up: How can I provide for myself and what will I do? Jesus. He is the manifestation of the invisible God. It's not about serving and getting a miracle. It is truly about him."

To make disciples is a heavenly calling that we all have as Christians. Heaven is in our hearts, and from that place we can minister to others. The Kingdom of God is an inheritance kept safe for us and a reward for what we've done for the Lord. It's not something we build here. Through many hardships we enter the Kingdom of Heaven. *Will I drop everything to get on my knees and worship the King of kings? Is he worthy of all of my affection and praise, or only worthy when I need a prayer answered or have a request? The Kingdom of God lives inside of me and I am called to preach the gospel to the ends of the earth.*

I sometimes wonder if Jesus, when he went to the cross, questioned God on whether he was making the best decision for him and if it was really going to be worth it to save a dying world who would continue to live a life of sin. Yet Jesus heard his Father so closely in everything because he abided and only did what he heard the Father say. Even though he didn't want to take the cup of suffering and he knew it was going to be painful, he knew that he could trust his Father and that he would be the living sacrifice for the sins of the world—All to the glory of God. So, the question is: *Is Jesus enough? Can I trust him in every area of my life or only the areas that I have previously had breakthrough in?*

Chapter 9

THE BUSH BUSH

The encounters that were happening in the school were unbelievable. The moment I would pick myself off of the ground was the moment when Holy Spirit would crash in with another word or revelation. This was a time of advancement and acceleration into the things of God. I was experiencing transformation through deep heart encounters with the Father that were stripping away all unwanted desires and things that were not of him. He was preparing me for my predestined calling, and he was going to send his Holy Spirit to speak to me about things that were unseen and unheard. He was getting ready to launch me and unveil the call for after Harvest School 30.

The next day in class, worship began and we were all in our "heavenly zones." We were typically scattered throughout the room freely moving in worship, but today we were asked to align in rows like a chain. Kurt and Will had locked arms with one another. Will had just prayed radical breakthrough over me as he walked down the aisle and put his hands on my head, and then Kurt came through. We were told to hold hands with the people on each side of us and start prophesying and praying out loud over one another. All of a sudden, I was praying for the guy next to me who was from Germany, and my entire body started shaking and I began to scream. I had never experienced anything like this before. I was overcome by the Spirit of God in intercession and travail.

As I screamed, it felt like a burning fire in my heart that was permeating my entire being and I couldn't stop. Flashes went through my mind where he showed me the streets of Los Angeles filled with the broken and lost. It was like a bad movie playing in my mind—a video with lost souls wandering all around. I knew I was going to the streets. My heart was burning with the love of Jesus for the orphaned and lost. I had never tangibly felt the pain of God's heart like I felt that day. God told me that there were going to be messengers of fire—angels to come along side of us. I could not breathe. I was slowly knocked down to my knees and then all the way to the floor. While there, God told me that I was destined to write, and that I was to write about his love. He would show me what to say.

Everything at Harvest School was lining up. We were taught about obedience and serving. I realized that sometimes when God speaks destiny over us, or when he speaks about the things he has prepared in advance, it's natural to analyze. I try to make sense of how this is going to work. *I don't even have a job to supply the needs of what you're calling me to do God*, I thought. But when he calls, there is always an abundance of provision for the call. He's calling us away from the things of the world and stripping away every idol that has attached itself and is not from him. Before I left for Harvest School, a great friend of mine said, "The call to go to Harvest School is great and I know you're giving up a lot, but the question I have is, are you going to be ready for the call that God speaks to you regarding what you're to do afterward?"

I think about this often and where I am now in life. The journey hasn't always been easy, but the relationships have been so valuable. The Bible talks about leaving our father and mother. The disciples left everything. The *yes* is powerfully worth it. We don't know what's behind the cost and the hills and valleys that we will face after we give God our *yes*, but the adventure with him is rewarding and in many cases, even fun. There is no better feeling than knowing that I am walking with him, beside him, and in him, in his perfect will and story for my life.

We were in the last couple of weeks of school, and every day, a student's life was transformed. During class one afternoon, Will walked up and down each aisle, releasing words and encouragement over us. There was much significance in what he said over me, "Beyond your wildest dreams, girl, beyond your wildest dreams." I could feel God's presence around me as he was hedging me in and preparing me for what was ahead in my life.

There was an opportunity to join the Harvest 30 dance team and perform a dance for the last day of class. When I was a kid, I always would ask my mom to sign me up for jazz, gymnastics, or some kind of extracurricular activity, but I often had struggled to feel good enough. I would practice for a few months and then would convince my mom that I needed to quit. I did not have any freestyle or prophetic dance experience other than jumping up and down and rallying all around filled with the Holy Ghost. I knew that in agreeing to participate in this dance, I would come face to face with some childhood stuff. God was inviting me to dance with him.

After our daily class was over, we had an outreach team meeting to discuss the logistics of our "bush bush" weekend outreach adventure. I had only heard of "the bush" before, referenced as a faraway land in the middle of nowhere. The "bush bush" was even further than what was known as the "bush." We were told by the leaders that the places we were going probably had never seen Caucasians, let alone heard about Jesus. Each team was assigned to different bush outreaches throughout Madagascar. The only information we were given was that we would be leaving Friday and returning on Sunday. There was no decision made on where we would be sleeping, nor did we know if there would be running water or bathrooms.

My detailed-oriented mind couldn't grasp the fact that there was not an exact plan of action or more details for the trip. I was in the twilight zone and could only hear the echoes of the sounds around me. After the meeting, the teams were excitedly jumping around, all pumped up to go on the bush bush outreach. I was absolutely terrified. I was scared to the same extent as I was the first day in Madagascar when I saw my room—in complete shock. I was scared to sleep in the middle of nowhere and with no running water or bathrooms. We didn't even know how long the van ride was going to be. It could be all night.

A lot of the students were sick, roaming the halls with stomach flu and diarrhea. My fears from the deepest places were haunting me as I began to think about this trip. I never went to places that didn't have bathrooms, and I needed to know everything. But I knew that this was part of the *yes*. Usually, I was the type of person who tried to know everything in advance, to best prepare and manage my expectations about what might or might not happen. I had to renew my mind and walk in my new nature in Christ.

During our entire mission trip, in his great love, he revealed to me how much fear and control that I was holding onto, and how it was still a stronghold in my life. When God wants to heal something, he does it from a place of love even if the situation seems completely unbearable. Satan likes to torment and make you feel like you haven't been forgiven or that you're still in bondage, but God so lovingly takes our hand and says, "I am with you and will help you walk through this thing that is still scary and real to you. I will never leave you or forsake you."

When I came to my room after the meeting, I felt completely discouraged and shaken up. I was crying, tears streaming down my face. My roommates Roberta and Heather were in the room and I told them what was going on. Roberta kneeled down on the ground beside my bed and began to pray. As soon as she started praying, Monica came bursting through the door. She said, "The Lord told me to come to the room and give you a hug." I couldn't believe the way the Lord sent my roommates to comfort me with his love. As we prayed and hugged, I could see in the spirit fear breaking off. Monica gave a word of breaking through and that this, indeed, was a time of overcoming. Roberta saw a picture of me walking on the stars and they were lighting up as I stepped on each one.

Monica then heard the Lord tell her to ask Roberta to sing over me. It was the most beautiful part of the moment. Roberta began to sing Steffany Gretzinger's song, *Out of Hiding*. I continued to weep. This song is so special to me. I immediately feel in a place of safety when I listen to it. Roberta then prophetically started singing the words and melody that the Holy Spirit gave her. The Lord took me to a place when I was a little girl. He showed me the first moment of my life when fear crept in and that in this moment, he was erasing all fear and trauma in the name of Jesus.

This is the song that Roberta sang over me:

I delight in you, my child
I delight in you
You'll never be alone
I'll never leave you

I delight in you, my child
I delight in you
I'm always with you
I'll carry you

When you feel like you can't stand
Then I'll be there too
As you walk upon the stars
You'll walk with confidence holding my hand

I delight in you, my child
I delight in you
Forever you are mine
And I'll always be with you.

This is the Body of Christ. Friends who champion and sharpen you. As I thanked God, my fear quickly turned into praise. I thanked him for loving me and leading me on this great adventure. I thanked him for the villages that we were getting ready to go to and that he had chosen me for such a time as this. I prayed for his overwhelming peace that surpasses all understanding. I prayed for our team that was going out and his protection over each and every one of us and the leaders. I prayed for the encounters, healings, and salvations for the people group that we would meet. Glory be to God who heals all of our diseases! I knew our team was going to be strong in the Lord.

We were heading out the next morning. I had packed everything that I was instructed to and the guys were loading up the vans. There had been so much anticipation leading up to this trip and yet the morning we were leaving everyone was sick and wandering around the hallways with some kind of food poisoning or flu. My cell phone had also completely stopped working right before it was time to leave and my battery would not hold a charge. I was freaking out because my entire plan to stay calm and listen to music on the bumpy ride to the bush bush was now going to be ruined if I couldn't charge my phone the entire weekend. Discouragement was settling in again, even before we left. But I had a real awareness that there was much opposition and pushback from the enemy to try to keep us from going on this trip. Nevertheless, we eventually split up into teams and left.

Our van ride to the bush bush was the bumpiest adventure that I had ever been on. We were smashed together two in each seat, and five or six hours later, we arrived at the house of a woman who was part of the village outreach. We walked in the dark through trails with flashlights to get to her home and when we did, we prayed over it and blessed her and her husband's ministry. We continued our journey and somehow, we made it down a rocky and bumpy road without blowing a tire. The driver accelerated the gas every hill that we went up, and we managed to arrive with only one small breakdown.

We arrived at the place we were staying, and there was no running water. We were going to be sleeping on the floor—no bed, no mirror or anything—so we laid down our sleeping bags next to each other and called it a night. A lot of the girls were really suffering from motion sickness from the ride and were throwing up nonstop. As bad as I felt for them, I was thankful for the grace God had given me and how he had used Israel bus rides to prepare me for the bumpy adventure in Madagascar.

The people at the church we were staying at were so kind and offered us something to eat before we settled in to sleep that night. But I couldn't bring myself to eat the food yet. The first night it was some sort of stew with meat. I had brought along some crackers and peanut butter packets just in case. In most cultures, it's extremely rude to not eat the food that is placed in front of you. My friend Taylor very kindly ate my food so it didn't go to waste. I was so thankful!

I slept really well the first night and used a latrine for the first time. The girls with experience on the mission field gave me some tips for squatting. I would hold my breath the entire time and then kick the door open when finished. It was very dark so someone would hold the flashlight through the crack of the door so that I could see. Some even wore headlamps. You didn't want to step in something that you weren't going to be able to wash off. We didn't have a sink to wash our hands either. One night down, and one more to go.

Unfortunately, the first night's meal before bed that I passed on made just about everyone sick and they were having to walk from the building where we were sleeping to the latrine in the middle of the night and didn't get much sleep. We all extended grace to one another as we knew that things were getting real and we were all human and loved each other.

The next morning, we split up into three teams to head out on foot to the nearby villages that my group was assigned to and we began the outreach and evangelism part of our trip. This village had never heard about Jesus. We stopped at many houses and places where people were gathering along the way and prayed for mothers and families. It was hard to minister because of the language barrier. The language in Madagascar is Malagasy, though some speak French. We had one translator with each team and a few of the students spoke French. This was my first time ministering with a translator, so I needed to pause a lot to let him translate after each sentence. I also was mindful of not bombarding the translator as if they were a puppet, knowing they were delivering the Word of the Lord.

Everywhere we stopped, children from that remote village would tag along and follow us from place to place. I couldn't believe it. The children ranged from age three months to around ten years. The young girls and boys carried their baby siblings swaddled on their back and followed us for miles with no shoes on. If the baby cried or needed to be swaddled again, the children would help each other and cater to the baby's need. The kids knew their way around the villages without any guidance.

Miracles were happening everywhere. A woman we prayed for was deaf and could now hear. We prayed for an oppressed man and the spirit of fear lifted off. There is power in the name of Jesus Christ. The sweetest thing was when a little girl with a baby on her back grabbed my hand and led me up a bumpy, red dirt hill, showing me the way to the other side of the hill. She was seven or eight years old. In that moment, I knew Jesus was leading me the entire time and my heart wept. I played Miss Mary Mack hand clap games with the kids and we sang songs.

God was getting rid of my fear of germs during this outreach. The kids with the runniest of noses and gunk all over their hands would grab a hold of my hand. My heart was so overwhelmed with his love for them that I didn't even care. I felt so comfortable and safe and I knew that he was there with us. We were in the middle of nowhere and somehow it felt familiar and peaceful. The same Holy Spirit that lives inside of me in my cozy home is the same one who lives in me across the world in Madagascar. While ministering in the next village, I received a word of knowledge. My elbow suddenly felt pain that I had never had before. I told the leader of the outreach about my elbow, as they were calling out words that the team was getting, and people received healing by faith. They asked if anyone had elbow or arm pain. A woman came forward who was experiencing shoulder pain and when we prayed, she was instantly healed. She lifted her arm above her head and waved it all around. Glory to God.

We walked to a nearby open field with a stage in the middle. Our team led a children's skit and we danced and sang. I passed out stickers, and the kids swarmed all of us, wanting everything that we had. After the skit, the babies were screaming for their mamas, and the children headed on their journey home. When the sun went down, we watched a film outside on the ground and stared up at the stars in amazement and wonder of how great our God is. Two people from my team got to share their testimony and extended an invitation for people to come and meet Jesus. We walked back to the building where we were staying. We had one more night and day before we headed back to our base.

The people we met while on the outreach were so kind and loving and really honored us while we were there. They even went out early in the morning and killed chickens so that we had food to eat. I eventually ate some of the food and it was really good. They always cooked some little rice patties that were savory or sweet called mofo gasy. They became my staple food in Madagascar. The hosts showed great honor and hospitality, working hard to serve our team. We then said our goodbyes and thanked everyone for hosting us. On the way home to our facility, the van broke down once again and some of the members from our team graciously hopped on the side of the road, eager to wait for another vehicle and flag it down. They had no idea when another van would be coming. I couldn't wait to get back to the place that I had once despised but actually was enjoying more and more.

This trip completely stretched me outside of my comfort zone, yet God gave me grace the entire way. I had peace in my heart. I cried when I returned safely to the facility because I was so overwhelmed with the love of God. I was so thankful for the many people we got to love on during the outreach and for the privilege of serving Jesus in this way.

The next morning during class, the leaders asked if anyone from our group wanted to share about their experience in the bush bush. I completely missed this moment because I was so sick that I couldn't stay out of the bathroom that morning. On our way back from the outreach we had eaten an interesting fish dish at a restaurant on the side of the road along with a Fanta drink that I later found out had been rebottled. My stomach wasn't having it anymore. When I came back to class, my friends said that everyone was looking for me to share because they knew that I had experienced such transformation. It was unbelievable grace to continue in a posture of worship and prayer even in a place of such adversity and sickness. If I were at home, I would have been in bed, but here, I was continuing to worship and give thanks to God.

The bush bush forced me out of my comfort zone and caused me to overcome my fears in a place of the unknown. I encountered God like never before and he met me in my weakness and made me strong in him.

Chapter 10

THE PERFECT PATH

The worship that takes place in Harvest School is supernatural. It's something I had never felt before and every single time we would press in and believe for a move of God, he would show up. Every night we would gather together after our days of outreach for a time of prayer, worship, and believing for what we had never seen before. We never knew how the Lord was going to show up in all of his glory on these nights. Many nights we would have an altar call where people would come up and be touched by the power of God and set free. Sometimes a word would be released over us and many people would be on the ground for hours receiving his love.

One night, the front of the room was in holy awe of the Lord Jesus while the back of the room was getting hit with the laughter and joy of the Lord. This night particularly, we were singing "How

Great Is Our God" and my mind was flashing to all of the amazing things that God had done in my life; I was catching glimpses of my history with him. Our history with God is so important. It is literally the story that he has written about us and we can partner with him in this. As I was singing, I realized that I never proclaimed how great my God was over my future. It was always reflecting back or in the present. But he is the one who was, the one who is, and the one who is yet to come. *What would it look like if I truly believed deep down that he was so great over everything that is yet to come?* I wondered. I could declare and prophesy things forth by speaking of his nature and who he is. So I began to prophesy, "You are great over my family, future, husband, marriage, children, finances, salvation, book writing, business, car, health, and grandchildren."

I asked myself: *What would it look like if I declared this every day from a place of thanksgiving and then trusted his sovereign will for my life? He is good over every single detail and he already has it figured out.* What an unbelievable revelation during this Holy Ghost party to worship and proclaim how great our God really is.

His love is sufficient. Have you ever just sat and let the Lord gaze into your eyes and tell you how beautiful you are to him? It's an exchange of his beauty through us in the mirror image of who he created us to be. During this exchange with him, he confirmed to me that I was exactly where I was supposed to be. I heard the Lord tell me as I sat at his feet everything that he loved about me. This was so special for me. When you come from a background of trauma, it's hard to receive sometimes when people tell you that you're beautiful or express how much you mean to them. It can be hard to understand if you've never considered yourself lovable or seen yourself in a loving way. But when God begins to speak about the way he sees you and his thoughts towards you, it melts away every fear, every doubt, and his love permeates every ounce of your being in such a loving fatherly way. He always proves his great love to us.

The next morning, Kurt shared a message that has impacted my life forever. Kurt, his wife Brooke, and his family led us so well on this Harvest School 30 mission trip. They represented the love of Jesus and what it looks like to do missions as a family. Kurt taught us to hear from God by getting into his presence. Kurt's family was called to the inner city and to an apartment that was scary, dangerous, unsafe, and looked completely opposite from the call of God on their life. He shared many personal testimonies about his family and how to stay steadfast and not be shaken. His message stirred hope and freedom.

Plan A or Plan B

Kurt said, "Everything might look so far away from what God said, but go to the location that he is sending you to and be the church." He was referencing that no matter where God takes us, we are to represent the church and the Body of Christ in that place. He told us how important it is to track with God and record what he says and the impressions or images of what he has laid on your heart. If you get a word, write it down. If someone confirms that word, write it down. You can hear from God by spending time with him, knowing his Word, and knowing his character. It can save you so much time when trying to make life decisions to discern his voice through hearing, knowing, and receiving wise counsel.

Kurt also instructed us that there will always be a temptation to think that Plan B is good enough. When God speaks, just be obedient, even when it doesn't feel good, and decree his presence wherever you are. He shared how, while on the field, they heard gunshots and saw so much shaking going on around them.

He continued, "When we are in the glory of God, it all makes sense. But when we are in the valley, we question God. It's helpful to take the pieces that you have and walk towards them even if you don't have all of them. Faith is all about walking in the unseen and believing for what you know the promises of God are for your life."

It confirmed for me that choosing to come to Harvest School was definitely God's Plan A for my life. I thank God for these surrendered men and women of God that hear his voice and go after it. If we can just do the one thing that he has said, it is a step in the right direction. Stewardship is so important and coming alongside people's vision to help build the Kingdom of God. Sometimes we are called to build something on our own and other times we are to simply come under a vision and support that. Plan A is the ultimate way and plan that God has written about us in his book of life.

"God has already given Moses provision for the valley," Kurt encouraged us. "Even though we don't know what the mountain looks like and how hard it is to go up and down, God already has it figured out. When we share our plan with people, we will receive pushback and others are not going to understand. Create a plan for what's to come and get ready for the new. Will you still believe when everything is absolutely crazy? God will give you a second chance and return the plan back to you. He will rewrite it so go back after it. God will connect the dots; we only need to show up and be available even when nothing makes sense."

Kurt shared how he kept going to pray in the streets of St. Louis that were full of crime. He told us that Plan A is a process and it takes time to build a team, receive provision, and know what God spoke to you on the mountain. Walking by faith also means we may not have all the pieces, but we can trust in an all-powerful, mighty God. "When things start shaking, you better know what God spoke to you on the mountain," he shouted. "It can take years and you might still not know what it looks like and that is okay. It's not about doing something, it's about being in his presence. During the times of waiting, the pressing and crushing begins. Not everyone is willing to wait on God's timing, so then they begin to pursue Plan B."

As I reflected on his teaching, I realized that God hadn't brought me all the way to Harvest School to have me turn around and do something man's way. I could have stayed at the nonprofit all summer in the office daydreaming away, and I'm sure things would have been fine. It was not the Plan A and path for me. It was only what I could temporarily see at the moment. God is a consuming fire and will have his way in our lives. He wants to use us and every detail for his glory. I knew that I had committed my ways to him and that he clearly was directing my path.

God began to speak to me more about the Plan A and vision moving forward after Harvest School. He gave me pictures of worship coming to the streets in Hollywood. He had been highlighting Los Angeles during the school, but now it was beginning to come alive as the visions were becoming very real. I saw churches in the streets being developed and books of testimonies coming from this movement. He was even showing me a guitar and a keyboard and said he was going to use my voice for this fresh wind coming. In this vision, he gave me a download for Hollywood and the Arts and Media. I saw him connecting me with the people and the culture. I also saw him building a team of worshipers, intercessors, and deliverers.

He began to speak to me about my obedience in prayer, intercession, and birthing the dreams that he had put into my heart. I heard him say, *"Come to me all who are weary, and I will give you rest. I am the resting place for the lost to be redeemed and forgiven. That the people shall be saved and reign in eternity forever with me and in my presence."*

The Garbage Dump

On one of our last days, we had a practical outreach and visited the local garbage dump where families live. I'd never seen anything quite like it before. There were tons of trash everywhere in the field, a little man-made lake, and a small village where people lived. Zebus, which are a type of cattle, pull the people with wagons of food, bricks for houses, and transportation. The garbage dump with the heaps of trash was directly next to the people's huts where they lived. It was really disheartening to see people digging through the dump and pulling out trash. The women sat in front of their makeshift houses and were stringing the clothing they salvaged like a harp to make colorful rugs to sell. The rugs were beautiful, and the Lord reminded me that he makes beauty from ashes.

The houses were made of muddy brick and plastic. Some had tin roofs, others had pieces of tarp as their covering. The kids were dressed in rags and torn clothing, while some were completely naked. They were covered in dirt and muck, with flies all over them. Some of the children were sitting in front of their homes eating handfuls of mush. It was deeply saddening to see the way that they lived in such extreme poverty.

We split into groups and went our separate ways to minister in their village. Some were in charge of the children's skits while others in my group were assigned to evangelize and pray for healing for the people and community there. I knew about three words in Malagasy, so translation was very important for us in order to communicate the gospel. We would pray in the Spirit constantly when we didn't have a translator. Holy Spirit knows every language. My group ran into three boys ages 11, 14, and 17 who wanted to be pastors. We prayed with them, and they asked to be filled with the Holy Spirit. They also had a lot of questions about hearing God's voice and the gifts of the Spirit. We prayed for fresh fire to fill them and also for one of the boys who had a hard time concentrating in school. He started praying in tongues immediately. It amazes me that we can be millions of miles away from home and all speak a different language, but in heaven there is one dialect—love.

We also saw a woman's sight restored and the swelling in a man's arms and his hand went completely down. There were many other miracles that day. When we were leaving, I saw some men floating around the lake on their makeshift boards, gathering mud for the bricks to build homes. I thought about how easy so many of us have it; that we can just use our house key and walk right into an air-conditioned home full of amenities, while these men and women were responsible for finding even the basic materials for building their house for shelter. As we left, we released a heartfelt blessing over the village.

The next day we went to children's church with the Malagasy kids and some local leaders. Don, my outreach team leader, asked if anyone wanted to share a testimony during church. I wasn't quite sure yet if the Lord was asking me to do this. Some of my friends were pumping me up but I wanted to make sure it was the Lord. We were all busy loading up the vans and getting ready to take off the next morning. No one volunteered to share, so I asked God if and what he wanted me to share and I felt like he said the Father's heart. I prayed for the kids and for God's heart for them as I prepared to share. When I looked up "father" in the concordance in the back of my Bible, God gave me 2 Corinthians 1:3-5 (NKJV): "Blessed be the God and Father of our Lord Jesus Christ, the Father of mercies and God of all comfort, who comforts us in all our tribulation, that we may be able to comfort those who are in any trouble, with the comfort with which we are ourselves are comforted by God. For as the sufferings of Christ abound in us, so our consolation also abounds through Christ."

This was my first time speaking since coming to Harvest School 30, and I had never spoken to a multi-generational crowd with a translator. It was a bit intimidating and also heavy on my heart when opening up about my relationship with my dad and God as my heavenly Father. God led me through, step-by-step as I spoke about his love and being a new creation in Christ. I shared the gospel and how Jesus died for each of us. I shared about adoption into sonship. I showered them with his love and let them know how much their heavenly Father cares for them. I personally found an even deeper meaning of his redemption by sharing about his love and how much I—and they—needed a savior.

God was really teaching me through this experience what it means to stand for him, stand for a nation, stand for a people, go after the lost, position my heart directly with him and minister to him so that everything else flows from that place. I knew that I would choose to live my life out of this place of rest and reliance.

God transformed my life through Harvest School 30. The speakers that came poured out their hearts and shared their testimonies of how they have laid down their life for the gospel. The power of

God that we experienced while there not only transformed us but set us apart.

I had many questions as we were beginning to wrap up our time. Would I continue to say *yes* when I headed back to Texas and be ready to partner with him for what was next? The reality that the school was ending and 103 of us would go back to our nations and homes was becoming very real and sad. I knew I was going back to something completely different than when I left. There were going to be a lot of changes and an entirely new living situation, but above all, I was different. The Lord was pulling things out of my heart that couldn't go with me into the next season. Doubt was one of those things. God was uprooting and clearing the way. I needed to be all in with no turning back.

Chapter 11

THE RAINFOREST

The rainforest was the final adventure for my outreach team before we left Madagascar. I'd always wanted to go to a rainforest and now was the chance to take a little break. I heard they had hot water in the showers which was very inviting since we had only showered in cold water the past three weeks. We loaded up the vans once again and took off into the unknown. I had much more peace about this trip than I'd had for the bush bush. I was excited about seeing the lemurs and all things tropical. We arrived safely and were given our room assignments and I had a new set of roomies for the weekend. The first night in the rainforest, I did not sleep well at all. It was freezing. I wondered, *What in the world is this canopy-looking drapery thing over my bed?* I later found out it was a mosquito net. Good thing we were still taking our malarial meds! It was so frigidly cold that I couldn't sleep with my head by the window and had to switch sides. The room was a creepy green with a white light that flickered on and off. Not a warm vibe. I had thought this was going to be so much better than what we had previously experienced. The Lord woke me up in the middle of the night to pray. I could feel the spiritual activity going on in the room.

I woke up not feeling well from being freezing cold all night and decided to opt out of the morning hike to hang with Jesus and friends in the café. It was raining and the outdoors are not particularly my favorite. God began to quicken my heart once again about complaining and grumbling about what things look like and to do everything without falling back into old habits and mindsets of the flesh.

> Live a cheerful life, without complaining or division among yourselves. For then you will be seen as innocent, faultless, and pure children of God, even though you live in the midst of a brutal and perverse culture. For you will appear among them as shining lights in the universe, offering them the words of eternal life. – Philippians 2:14-16 (TPT)

I got to see the alligators and the lemurs on the afternoon trip. We fed the lemurs bananas and they would jump up on our shoulders. The first one devoured the banana so quickly out of my hands I thought he was going to eat my hand off too. We took a paddle boat across the stream to get back to the other side. Our teams were becoming so close. I was becoming a professional squat latrine user and was loving all of the snacks that I hadn't allowed myself to eat in years. I experienced so much grace the whole two months to be myself and live free from perfectionism, control, and condemnation.

I connected more closely with some of the leaders the last few days and they gave me many words of wisdom and direction. Once we got back from the rainforest trip, I met with my house mom to debrief about our time in Harvest School. She saw a great transformation in my life and shared about my ability to change and influence atmospheres. She prophesied that what I carried changed the room, so I needed to pay attention to what I was carrying and partnering with. One thing I had realized from being in so many different atmospheres and places was that I was definitely a feeler and needed to be aware so that I could pray. She continued to bless and honor me for being deeply rooted in my walk with the Lord and acknowledged the struggles I had experienced. The stretching in Harvest School was by far the most challenging journey I had ever faced before.

The next morning, Mama Pamela taught a class and encouraged us that nothing is wasted with God and that our whole life is an offering to him poured out until we meet face to face in eternity. There were so many tangible biblical examples from Exodus to Mark about how his presence will go with us, and that we can choose to sit at his feet like Mary did. She shared about her life that had been rooted in trauma, and how Jesus wants to give us a white stone with our new name and break away every label that people or our family have put on us, so we can step into all that God has. When we are born again, Jesus comes to make all things new in us and through us and it's never too late to give our lives to him. There's nothing that can disqualify us from living our best life with Jesus. She reminded us that our value is not in our performance. Our identity doesn't come from a title and what job we have. It is not a checklist but a love affair with Jesus.

Our last teaching of the school was from Pastor Surprise about territorial anointing. I had no idea the impact that this teaching would render and how it became the launching and alignment for my ministry today. He said that whenever we go to the places where God calls us to go, he is giving us a territorial anointing for that place, and when we are called to a place, there is always a group of demons that come alongside who try to keep us from truly fulfilling the call of God in that region. He continued to teach us that when we pray for a place, we must pray for a territorial anointing. We can pray to recognize the angels where we are. When God is promoting us to the next level, he will remove certain people from our lives and when he is blessing us, he will bring the people into our lives to help carry out the vision. He said to us, "When God encounters you, he will come to you in a way that will give you direction and he will come in a way that you don't expect it."

He asked each of us to stand and declare and claim the land that we were taking. He said to declare the anointing over that city. Even though my residence was still in Fort Worth, Texas, and I knew that I would be going back to Ohio to visit family, God had shown me Hollywood and the city of Los Angeles when I was commissioned out of Galilee by Heidi Baker. The impression in my spirit was very strong that God was sending me to claim the land in California for his glory. I stood up in front of the group and claimed ground over Ohio, Texas, and California. It sounded a bit nuts that I was shouting multiple places in the United States when others were declaring other nations. But I had always known since my time at the evangelism school that North America was my mission field for now.

Pastor Surprise told us that the place he was called to minister was the place he was called to prepare. He shouted, "You better know who you are and who you are not!" This ministered to my heart so much. John the Baptist was preparing the way for Jesus. "Believe the words that he has spoken over your life," he declared. We can defend ourselves or simply rest in who Jesus says we are. John was doing it all for Jesus. *God must become greater so that I can become less. When people see me whether it's in ministry, marketplace, family, or on the streets, I can point them to Jesus. They believed because of John's testimony. I want to burn like this and have such a heart for the people, that they will only see Jesus.*

Chapter 12

THE DANCE

It was Harvest School 30 graduation day! I had been practicing faithfully with the dance team in between our daily teachings and outreach. It was showtime! We were dressed in all black and I had the entire routine memorized. I was excited to dance for Jesus. At the beginning of the routine, the music changed, and we re-enacted Ezekiel 37 as we turned into dry bones lying flat on our backs on the floor. Then the Holy Spirit blew through the land over the dry bones and we started to come alive as we moved ourselves back to our feet. When I hit the floor as dry bones, my right knee stayed bent when it should have been flat on the floor. I wanted to lay it down as soon as I noticed I messed up, but there wasn't time. I had messed up! My heart was racing. I couldn't believe it. Immediately the enemy made me feel like a failure. But in God's graciousness, I heard him say, "I am breaking off this perfectionist spirit and a spirit of performance" and that he was proud of me. He also told me to not make any mention of this to the dance team. I was not to condemn myself for not performing up to my own standards. God spoke to my heart and said, *See yourself the way that I see you. Love yourself the way that I love you. Have compassion on yourself the way that I have compassion for you. You will no longer criticize or condemn yourself because in that you are condemning me. You will love yourself and see yourself as beautiful because I see you as beautiful and you are mine.* We finished the dance to our Harvest 30 anthem and invited the school up as we broke out in worship and shouts unto the Lord.

We headed into the back room when we finished and many of the girls were saying how they had forgotten certain parts of the dance and how they messed up. I smiled and thanked God for his goodness. Don't discredit the small. I received victory and the breaking of the perfectionist spirit even on my last day in Madagascar. It was beautiful.

During worship, I had a vision where Jesus grabbed my hand and asked me to come with him to the edge of the mountain, and then we jumped off together. It felt like I was free falling with him. He said, "We are going low and you are going to be leaving more behind. The ground will be hard, but it will eventually soften and I am paving the way." In that moment, I was standing in the very center of the students during the worship and he said, "You are in the center of my will. You are in the center of my love."

As the worship team sang, "Jesus you're beautiful, Jesus you're beautiful," I was so overwhelmed by the beauty of Jesus and his love for people near and far, my fellow classmates, and everyone in between. I was completely undone by his love. He cares so much about each person, every tribe and tongue, and I couldn't even begin to grasp his goodness and faithfulness as he encountered every individual in a tangible way that transformed their hearts. He had molded us together in his image in a corporate way as the Body of Christ and as classmates from 26 different nations. He set us apart and called us each by name to go to Scotland, Israel, and Madagascar. He joined us together as a family for such a time as this to worship the King of Glory and all his splendor. He called us away with him. The beauty and wonders of his love are unfathomable.

Kurt gave us a final word of encouragement speaking truth and life over our school, and shared how much we blessed the staff and leaders. He told us to keep our eyes on the invisible and reassured us that we were going to be okay. As we made a commitment that day to step into the new and to never look back, we knew that we would never be the same. No more complaining. God had taken the orphan spirit from us.

"We are at the starting line," Kurt said. "It's not a sprint of perseverance but a race of endurance by faith, keeping our eyes on Jesus. God is the champion who initiates and perfects our faith."

I wrote in my journal: *We don't cross over and then say we want to go back. We have to put our name to what God is calling each of us to do in the next chapter. What he is calling us to do is impossible without him and without people in this room.*

The relationships we had built were truly of a family and of one accord. God had deposited so much in us during these two months that we didn't even realize all that was in our account. We definitely saw things we had never seen before. We moved so quickly from glory to glory and one encounter to the next. From baptisms in the Jordan to shouting in the heavenly rooms of glory with children prophesying and others falling down drunk in the Spirit. We literally had to carry friends out of the gatherings because they were on the ground undone by his love. When we entered the fire tunnels, we never came out the same.

As I contemplated all that had happened, I wrote down my final notes. *It doesn't matter who is with me when I go home, I still need to do what Jesus is calling me to do. I need to continue to run the race. In that, I have everything that I need and can give away everything I've been given to the next person. Will I do something with what he's given me? What am I doing today for Jesus? It's time to take the baton and go! We have been commissioned from the Father's heart to run and to abide in him in such a deep place of his obedience and steadfast love for us. In him, I can have life. I have everything that I need and know exactly who I am in him where everything is perfected and made holy and righteous in the image of Jesus who gave his life for me. He is a God of miracles. I have received through Harvest School 30 the robe of righteousness, the ring of the Holy Spirit, and the golden chain which represents the wisdom of God. My future is bright in him, and he who has called me is faithful to fulfill the purposes in Christ Jesus. Amen*

What We've Never Seen Before

Harvest School 30 Anthem
Written by Harvest School 30 Staff

Oh, my heart cries out to you
All my praise, all my praise is due

For your name is my strength and tower
To your name be all glory and power

Every dream every vision everything that we've thought
All the things that you've placed in our hearts
Would you come would you unlock the doors to them all
Would you unlock the doors to our hearts

We say yes to you, Jesus
We'll go there for you
All the places we haven't gone before
The places that are new

We say yes, yes, yes, yes

Stay strong, my child
I'm giving you faith
Stay strong, my child
I'm giving you faith

We believe we'll see what we've never seen before
We believe, we believe
We believe
(Stay strong, my child/ I'm giving you faith)
We believe we'll see what we've never seen before
We believe, we believe

I'm faithful, I'm steadfast; you know who I am
Who you are in me
Is faithful to the end

We believe, we believe
What we've never seen before

Chapter 13

THE ADVENTURE WITH GOD CONTINUES

Harvest School ended in August 2019. I flew back to Fort Worth to my host family, Carol and Daryl's home, and reacclimated back to society. It took me a couple of weeks to adjust to all of the amenities and luxuries we have living in the United States. I went home to visit my family in Ohio for a few weeks and kept my stuff in storage in Texas for a bit.

Before I flew to Ohio, I had the impression to Google the name Mel Tari. He was Rolland's friend and I saw that he had written a book called *Like a Mighty Wind*. I decided to buy his book and took it with me to Ohio. In the book he mentioned that he couldn't wait to get to America since he was from a small island, Timor, in Indonesia. He thought America was the land where everyone trusted in God. I found it interesting that the first place he arrived was Los Angeles. When the plane touched down in LAX, he thought the devil had landed him in the wrong place. Everywhere he walked he saw dirty looks, liquor and bars, and people smoking. He needed God's help. I now can see what he was referring to when God calls us to a land that we think is a certain way and it looks completely different than what we had imagined.

Throughout the weeks of visiting my family, my heart continued to stir with the visions God had given me in Harvest School about going to the streets of Los Angeles. The first Sunday home, I visited the missions-based church, Frontline International. They were having an upcoming conference in October and Mel Tari was one of their speakers. I decided to extend my trip and stay for the conference. Mel prayed and prophesied over me during one of the breakout sessions and said, "This is the beginning of the journey with Jesus and God already has it figured out for you. Even 40 years from now." He continued, "Moses ran away from Egypt and 40 years later he had the encounter in the burning bush and it literally changed the destiny of millions of people taking them from the land of bondage to the promised land." He blessed me for years to come, and all the years in between, and said that I have taken a journey that I will never regret because I have made the decision to follow. He said, "Remember—this day is just the beginning of an eternal journey with Jesus. We bless you and release you into the fullness of your destiny in the name of Jesus."

Before Harvest School 30, I attended the "Light the Fire" conference in Toronto, where I met a couple named Mark and Mona. We had kept in touch throughout my time in the school, and we talked often when I returned. I shared with Mona what God had spoken to me about California and India when I was commissioned out of Galilee. She and her husband lived outside of Los Angeles and had a nonprofit in India, which I had no idea about. This connection was really important. As I continued to sense an urgency from God to go to the place that he kept showing me with lost people in the streets, I decided to schedule a trip to Los Angeles for a few days and see what this was all about. Mark and Mona extended the offer to host me during my trip to Los Angeles. This was very caring and trusting of them since we only had briefly met at the conference in Toronto. I had only been to Los Angeles one other time, seven years prior, when I first came to know the Lord. When I was younger, I had wanted to be a public relations specialist and interview movie stars on the red carpet. I had forgotten about this dream once I got saved because my reality TV days and worldly ways of thinking and living were far over. This was something that God was bringing back around to use for his glory.

My friend Monica from Harvest School lived outside of Los Angeles in Orange County, and my close friend, Paul, who was part of my outreach team, was near Los Angeles as well. A couple of friends that were part of Harvest School 30 had previously told me about their short-term mission trips to the Dream Center. The Dream Center is a large nonprofit organization in Los Angeles that serves as a resource and provides support to those affected by homelessness, hunger, addiction, and lack of education, and it has many residential and outreach programs. The Angelus Temple is the church of the Dream Center located in Echo Park.

After several months of Googling the Dream Center, I saw they had a job opening for a marketing manager. I really wanted to do inner city missions and loved street evangelism, praying for the lost, helping people get connected to resources that could help them—but I wondered how this "rescue call" on my life would connect with helping the homeless find somewhere to live and getting them the help that they needed. I cleaned up my resume and cover letter and was going to apply for the job at the Dream Center.

As I was working on my paperwork, I kept scanning the Dream Center website and came across a program called "Immersion" which was a hands-on, missions-based opportunity to serve and live amongst the people who were part of the residential rehabilitation program, leadership school students, families, staff, and more. The cafeteria feeds the people from the streets, and there are many programs and ministries that serve the entire Los Angeles area. The Immersion program had different tracks that you could choose from as part of the residential and outreach programs.

That night, I began to contemplate this program while I also had hopes in my plan to submit my resume and cover letter the next day. When I woke up the next morning to apply, the job position that had been posted for months was gone from the website. I love when God closes doors and directs me in the way that I should go. Since I was going to be visiting Los Angeles, I reached out to the Dream Center tour director to see if they could do a tour with me while I was in town the next week. Unfortunately, they had an event that day and couldn't do it. The day before I left, which also marked the end of my 40-day fast, the director of Immersion reached out to me and offered to take me around the campus, which was miraculous timing.

I traveled to Los Angeles to see my friends Mark and Mona and got to meet many people. We went to Hollywood to pray and evangelize on the streets. I joined with a couple friends for a school outreach and got to pray for students. The presence of God was so strong everywhere I went. My friend Monica and I drove through Skid Row so I could see what it looked like. Paul took me to the Pasadena International House of Prayer (PIHOP) which, since then, has become a monumental place for me to seek the Lord. It was such a powerful time of new friendships, ministry, and pressing into God's heart.

In the midst of the busyness, new ministry connections, and many opportunities to serve, I also felt God challenging me. "Jackie, you can do ministry all day long and still be far from me." This really shifted the posture of my heart from a place of doing for God to a place of abiding in God.

When I was getting ready to head back to Texas, I was at the LAX airport when I heard the Lord say that his favor would be upon me if I moved to Los Angeles. When I got on the plane and we took off, tears began to stream down my cheeks because I knew that this was it. Once again, I would be traveling to the land that he showed me. It reminded me of what my friend asked me before I left for Harvest School: Would I be willing to go to the place that God was asking me to go after the school?

I arrived back in Texas. The next morning, I immediately called my mom and told her about my encounter with God and asked if I could move my remaining stuff out of storage to her house in Ohio. She kindly agreed and couldn't believe I was going to move to Los Angeles. God reminded me that I had kept seeing the numbers 648 before I left for Harvest School. I suddenly realized why. This was my mom's address where I would be sending my stuff while in Los Angeles.

I reached out to the Immersion Director, who took me on a tour, and then I applied by faith for the program. I planned to go home for the holidays and spend time with my family before heading out to the Dream Center to jump into inner city missions. I was preparing to go (in the same way I began reading the Harvest School books) even though I hadn't been accepted into Immersion yet. The director even offered me the option to do two tracks (residential and outreach) which had never been done before, and to be part of the adopt-a-block outreach program and the women's rescue residential program. This was exactly what I had wanted to do in my heart, and I knew this was the open door to go through. I hired a moving company to move my stuff from Texas storage to Ohio and after Thanksgiving, I said my goodbyes to my lovely friends, host family, and church family in Texas.

I still hadn't been accepted yet to the program but I was believing that God was lining everything up. The movers were two weeks late on delivering my stuff to Ohio. Finally, the day after my things arrived, I received the call that I had been accepted into the Immersion program starting January 13, 2020. The next morning, I was looking through my labeled boxes in my mom's basement, trying to find the one that had my heating blanket in it since it was winter in Ohio. I found the box and when I opened it up there was something wrapped up in packing paper. When I unraveled it, it was my Hollywood coffee mug that I had purchased years prior. God confirmed to me through this that Hollywood was exactly where I was to go. I had no idea before going to Harvest School that God would be speaking to me about going to Hollywood, and this was the first item I opened seven months later.

In January 2020 before the pandemic, I packed up all my stuff into two suitcases and flew to LAX where my friend Monica picked me up. We headed to the Dream Center the following day. When I saw where I was moving and the neighborhood where I would be living, it reminded me of Mel Tari's experience when he touched down in Los Angeles. Somehow, it looked different than what I had remembered on the tour. The main building was huge, and there were multiple buildings on the campus that were concrete and a bit old-looking. Years ago, the campus was the Queen of Angels Hospital. Little did I know that when I said *yes* to Los Angeles to do full-time missions, that we were getting ready to enter into a worldwide pandemic and all that would happen within the next year. God was training me in so many ways and preparing me for battle. I was learning the culture, principalities, and people in Los Angeles. It was much different than Ohio, Texas, or anywhere else I had lived.

Inner city missions at the Dream Center was one of the best and most pressing times of my life. While there, I got to love on people who were young and old, have Bible studies at the park, serve food to families and seniors door-to-door during the pandemic. On Sundays, we would pick up people in Skid Row and take them to church with us. I started a Bible study with a woman who lived in a tent at the park. For the next three months, we saw many hearts changed and people delivered and transformed. The Lord spoke to me during my time and told me that the Dream Center was the hub to get me to where he was taking me to. Mark and Mona continued to support me and were always safe people I could go to and hang out with since I didn't have family in California. God always sent people and he always provided for every single one of my needs.

I never went without food, shelter, and provision even though I hadn't worked in many months. My time in Immersion got extended from July to September because of the pandemic and not being able to serve in my two tracks. Church shut down at the Angelus

Temple so we could only watch it online. When I first arrived to Los Angeles, my mentor had told me about the Hollywood House of Prayer (HOP) and church called Radiance International. Radiance is an Apostolic Center situated right in the arts and entertainment capital of the world, Hollywood. It is a hub for marketplace business, music, works of justice, and campus awakening. In July 2020, with every church shut down besides Radiance, I was able to start attending. The church reminded me of my apostolic churches in Texas and Ohio and was very Spirit-filled. I deeply desired to be planted in a church community again and to have close family relationships like I previously had.

After many months of serving during some very intense situations—Covid, protests and riots, helicopters circling looking for criminals, not being able to leave the campus and having a curfew mandated by the city among other things—I was ready for a change. I really needed rest and peace in my living situation. I missed my family and friends and wasn't able to travel home because of the quarantine and isolation. I was praying about what I was going to do after Immersion and whether or not I should finish out 2020 at the Dream Center or not. That night before bed, I prayed and asked God what I should do as I presented the options he was revealing to me. Then I sat still before him to hear what he was saying. When I prayed about Radiance International, I felt the presence of God so strongly come over my body as I was sitting on my bed. The next morning when I woke up, I received an email from the Pastors, Jonathan and Sharon Ngai, inviting me to meet up so they could get to know me and hear my story. I also wanted to learn more about them and Radiance's ministry. We met up about a week later and had a wonderful time. They shared about an open space in a room above the HOP that had just become available. We were all going to take time and pray about it. As I began to scroll and look up other places in the area, I felt the conviction of the Holy Spirit that I was to move to West Hollywood to be closer to the ministry and share the room. The Ngais felt the same, and I agreed to move in by September 1.

Immersion was wrapping up, the lovely lady who I did Bible study with was put into a hotel by the state and got off the streets, and the Lord was transitioning me out of the Dream Center and to the Sunset Strip in West Hollywood. I couldn't believe it. Since I had given up my car before Harvest School, I spent the first eight months in Los Angeles with no car walking the streets. God miraculously provided a car for me in Ohio at my stepdad's dealership and used a very special lady to bless me to get it. I bought the car in June but knew that I wasn't supposed to bring it to Los Angeles until August even though I had no clue why. When August came around, a dear friend was praying, and felt the Lord tell him to pay to have my car shipped from Ohio to Los Angeles. I couldn't believe it. The car truly was the blessing that God used to get me from the hub to the place that he was taking me to—Hollywood.

I finished out my time well at the Dream Center. My director even blessed me with things that I needed for my new place and I made so many great relationships there. I loved getting to serve the city and it was hard for me to shift into something else because the ministry the Lord had given me was really taking off. I was very content walking the streets and loving on the people. But I had to be obedient to where he was asking me to go.

I was all settled in a shared room on the third story above the HOP and was starting to unwind from all that I had experienced since I moved to Los Angeles. The pastors called a meeting with me and shared more about their vision and heartbeat for Radiance and told me that their administrator of eight years was moving. They knew that I had an administration and ministry background from our first meeting and kindly offered me the Executive Administrator part-time position at Radiance. I was very honored and agreed to fully step into this role and space that the Lord had prepared for me.

A week after moving, I was driving down the Sunset Strip one morning when I tried turning left and a guy ran the traffic light and smashed my car. A man who was homeless came running out into the intersection to make sure I was okay, since my airbag deployed and my face hit the steering wheel. By the grace of God, I was not hurt other than a beat-up thumb, and he stayed there with me the entire time to serve as a witness, even though in California they don't cite you and it's up to the insurance. I could not believe after all that had been involved into getting this car from Ohio to Los Angeles, it was now totaled only after a couple of weeks. I could sense the warfare and opposition going on the second I touched down in that area. Because of God's favor, the insurance agency called the witness and his statement saved me from being faulted. The adjuster loved the work I did in Los Angeles and gave me double for what I paid for the car since I got such a great deal from my stepdad's dealership. Since I had just become employed, and have good credit, I was able to go to a dealership and apply for a leased car. God blessed me with a brand-new car with all the bells and whistles to safely get me around town.

I was obedient and heard the call of God to go to Hollywood, a call which had been confirmed through the dreams and the vision he had given me in 2019 during Harvest School as well as many other confirmations. After I answered the call, I immediately went into a six-month wilderness period that started with the car accident. At times I struggled with loneliness, adjusting to various responsibilities, and building new relationships. It was also a very intense living situation on the Sunset Strip. The Sunset Strip is known for its iconic music venues, nightclubs, restaurants, and tourist attractions; however, it also has a very dark side. I was surrounded by people screaming, getting high, partying, and witchcraft. Even trying to get to a grocery store was a challenge. The way of life here was so different than what I was used to. It was very fast—fast cars, fast people. The car accident threw me for a loop, as I had to get back out on the road again. I then became very sick with Covid for a long time and my mental health was under extreme attack. I seldom slept and was up almost every night because of the loud music and mayhem going on outside. One night I woke up to grenades and military troops outside of my window because of the protests going on—the presidential election stirred up a lot on the streets and I was living right in the middle of it.

Only God. God used this time to establish and to strengthen me in him. He healed even deeper layers and caused me to stand when all I wanted to do was run. He trained me how to pray, seek his face, read my Bible even more and stay abiding in him. I became so weak that only in him could I become strong.

I found favor in the Lord's eyes, and once my "training bootcamp" in Hollywood was over, things began to shift. I began to see incredible fruit come forth from the visions that I saw during Harvest School. On New Year's Eve 2021, Sean Feucht and "Let us Worship" came to the streets of Los Angeles in Skid Row, Azusa, Echo Park, Angelus Temple and Aimee Semple McPherson's home. They brought prophetic acts of worship, dancing, and praise to the Lord. I believe this was a prophecy fulfilled from the visions that

I previously had when I saw worship coming to the streets of Los Angeles.

There have been teams of intercessors and worshipers, tent revival meetings, and deliverance in the park in Hollywood. God has connected me with the Arts and Entertainment through Radiance International. He also has connected me in the marketplace again. It's wondrous to see the things God has done and brought forth even in my obedience to finally write this book. I am seeing all the puzzle pieces come together of his marvelous goodness and how he works everything together for good for those who love him and who have been called according to his purpose. I'm thankful for every season, each place I've lived, and the opportunity to serve God in this way.

Final Thoughts

The journey doesn't always look like what we think it will. The wilderness is the preparation season after the call if we will only stand and let him establish us in him. I can trust that no matter what each season looks like, he never changes. I never thought in a million years that when I said *yes* to coming to Los Angeles to do inner city missions, that this was what the journey would look like. I am forever changed, grateful, and realize that I can do nothing apart from him. He is my strength to even be able to drive through the hills and valleys, highways and byways. God is the only one who can do these things. He has provided abundantly beyond anything that I can think or imagine. I came out here with two suitcases and he has completely built my life. He has given me a safe and beautiful home to live in. I'm so thankful for the friends and family who have supported me, my church family, and the journey of God's love here in California. He is so worthy of everything, all of our time, affection, belongings, and life. He always gives so much more than what we give up and is always faithful. He truly directed my steps to get to Los Angeles, Hollywood, and connected it all to where I am now.

I also can't imagine what I would have missed out on if I hadn't said *yes* to Harvest School 30. I would never be where I am now. The lives that have been changed and relationships that have been built through my obedience have made it more than worth it. People have come to know Jesus and have been healed, delivered, and discipled. They have felt the love of God and have hope again. At times, it was very hard for me to tread in the water, and I could not see what it was going to look like with my natural eyes, but God gave me more faith to trust in him and believe in the promises that he has spoken over me. I have hope in Jesus Christ; even though we can't see him, we love him and we know his grace is more than enough. I can continually pour out my life unto him because he is worthy of all of the honor, all of the glory, and all of the praise.

> But those who wait on Yahweh's grace will experience divine strength. They will rise up on soaring wings and fly like eagles, run their race without growing weary, and walk through life without giving up. – Isaiah 40:31 (TPT)

It's Never Too Late to Say Yes to Jesus

If you do not have a personal relationship with Jesus Christ and would like to enter into knowing him and have the gift of eternal life, you can pray this prayer. Jesus gave his life so that you can live free from all bondage, strongholds, fear, and have abundant life on this earth. Giving my life to Jesus was the best decision I've ever made. Let's pray this prayer together and invite Jesus into your heart:

> Jesus, I know that I am a sinner and that I have lived a life far from you. I am sorry for all of the sins I've committed, people that I've hurt, unbelief, and doing whatever I have wanted to do. I turn from my sin right now, I repent, and I accept you today as Lord and Savior of my life. I invite you into my heart, into my life, and into every circumstance from this day forward. I want to live for you, Jesus. I want to have eternal life with you. Thank you for dying on the cross for me. Thank you that I can experience freedom today because of what you did for me on the cross. I accept your love, grace, and forgiveness of my sins. I choose to follow you today and to never turn back. Fill me, Holy Spirit, with the fullness of who you are. I love you and thank you that I can have eternal life and an abundant life on this earth with you today and forever. In Jesus' Name. Amen. (Romans 3:23; Romans 6:23; Romans 5:8, Ephesians 2:8-9; Romans 10: 9-10)

Saying YES to God Again

Lord, I surrender my plans to yours. You are worthy of my every desire, every thought, every decision, and where I go in this life. It is no longer I who live, but Christ who lives in me. I commit myself again to you today, Jesus, and I say have your way. I say *yes*. I thank you that I get to journey with you on this great adventure. You have the *yes* of my heart. In Jesus' name. Amen (Galatians 2:20)

ABOUT THE AUTHOR

Jacquelyn May has a Bachelor of Arts Degree in Applied Communication from Kent State University and is a certified Mental Health Coach. She is also a member of Christ for All Nations Evangelism Alliance.

She started off in medical education where she was part of building the department of Faculty Affairs for two-start up medical schools. She was the Director of Faculty Affairs at TCU and UNTHSC School of Medicine. She then transitioned into the nonprofit sector in development to raise money for the programs for women, children, and families.

In 2019, Jackie attended Iris Global Harvest School 30, where she received her call to missions. In 2020, she moved to Los Angeles to serve at the Dream Center and minister through inner city evangelism, park Bible study, and women's rescue missions.

Presently, Jackie serves as the Executive Administrator at Radiance International Church in Hollywood. She is also part of intercession teams and marketplace ministry. She is passionate about healing, evangelism, and discipleship—seeing people walk freely in their identity and purpose in Christ.

Made in the USA
Monee, IL
11 November 2021